Lecture Notes of the Institute
for Computer Sciences, Social Informatics
and Telecommunications Engineering 15

Kandeepan Sithamparanathan
Mario Marchese (Eds.)

Personal
Satellite Services

International Conference, PSATS 2009
Rome, Italy, March 18-19, 2009
Revised Selected Papers

 Springer

Volume Editors

Kandeepan Sithamparanathan
Broadband and Wireless Group, Create-Net
via alla Cascata 56 D, 38100 Trento, Italy
E-mail: kandeepan@ieee.org

Mario Marchese
Universita of Genova
Department of Communications
Computer and System Sciences
via Opera Pia, 13, 16145 Genova, Italy
E-mail: mario.marchese@unige.it

Library of Congress Control Number: 2009933643

CR Subject Classification (1998): C.2, E.3, J.2, K.6.5, C.2.5, J.1

ISSN   1867-8211
ISBN-10   3-642-04259-7 Springer Berlin Heidelberg New York
ISBN-13   978-3-642-04259-1 Springer Berlin Heidelberg New York

springer.com

© ICST Institute for Computer Science, Social Informatics and Telecommunications Engineering 2009
Printed in Germany

Typesetting: Camera-ready by author, data conversion by Scientific Publishing Services, Chennai, India
Printed on acid-free paper   SPIN: 12731312   06/3180   5 4 3 2 1 0

PSATS 2009 Conference Report

The International Conference on Personal Satellite Services 2009 (PSATS 2009) was held at the Sheraton Golf Di Medici, Rome, Italy during March 18–19, 2009, jointly organized by the ICST (Belgium),Create-Net (Italy), SAT Expo (Italy) and Eutelsat (France).

The PSATS 2009 scientific conference was co-located with the Space Applications and Technologies exhibition event (SAT Expo Europe) in Rome during March 19–21, 2009. On first day (18th March) of PSATS several high-quality technical and scientific papers were presented, and the second day of the conference was collocated with the SAT Expo event at the Fiera Roma stadium, in Rome, Italy.

The conference included a keynote speech, one invited presentation and 19 scientific paper presentations spanning over four technical tracks. One of the tracks was a special session (workshop) on "Performance Enhancing Proxies for Internet Application over Satellites." The Keynote speech was given by Saitto Antonio, Director of Innovation and Technology at Telespazio Rome-Italy, titled "Satellite Technology: From Sky Down to Earth for a Sustainable Development". The invited talk was presented by Giuseppe Conti, a senior research scientist from the Fondazione Graphitech, titled "Future Satellite Location-Based System: Intelligent Transport System for Optimized Urban Trips." Both presentations, from Telespazio and Graphitec, were well received and discussed among the participants.

The workshop on "Performance-Enhancing Proxies (PEP)" was organized in collaboration with the ETSIBroadband Satellite Multimedia (BSM) group and the European Satellite Communications Network of Excellence (Satnex) by Dr. Haitham from the University of Surrey.

Eutelsat's participation at the conference and the influence throughout the organization of the PSATS 2009 event was quite significant, and also considered to be a key contributing factor to the success of this event, along with the prominent contributions from ICST, SAT Expo, and Create-Net.

The conference had participants both from the industrial and the academic sectors from various parts of the world such as Japan, France, and the UK. The venue of the event 'The Sheraton Gold, Roma' was definitely a wonderful place to have a conference.

Finally, I would like to thank the Organizing Committee members, the Technical Program Committee members and all the reviewers who contributed immensely toward the success of this event. Also, on behalf of the Organizing Committee and the Steering Committee of PSATS, I would like to thank the ICST, Create-Net, SAT Expo and Eutelsat for their extended support in making this event a successful one, and I very much look forward to seeing even more successes in 2010 and the forthcoming years for PSATS.

S. Kandeepan

Organization

Steering Committee

Imrich Chlamtach (Chair)	President, Create-Net, Italy
Kandeepan Sithamparanathan	Create-Net, Italy
Hongfei Du	Simon Fraser University, Canada
Agnelli Stefano	Eutelsat, France

Conference General Chair

Zhili Sun	University of Surrey, UK

Conference General Co-chairs

Kandeepan Sithamparanathan	Create-Net, Italy
Hongfei Du	Simon Fraser University, Canada

Technical Program Committee Co-chairs

Mario Marchese	University of Genoa, Italy
Giovanni Corazza	University of Bologna, Italy

International Advisory Chairs

Alexander V. Sergienko	Boston University, USA
Sam Reisenfeld	University of Technology Sydney, Australia

Publicity Chair

Agnelli Stefano	Eutelsat, France

Advisory Committee Chairs

Paolo Dalla Chiara	President Sat Expo, Italy
Renata Guarneri	Create-Net, Italy

Conference Coordinator

Robert Varga   ICST, Belgium
Gladys D. Chiara   Satexpo, Italy
Ilaria Pivato   Satexpo, Italy

Publication Chair

Yan Zhang   Simula Research Laboratory, Norway

Website Chair

Lorenzo Mucchi   University of Florence, Italy

Track Chairs

Sudharman Jayaweera   University of New Mexico, USA
Radoslaw Piesiewicz   Create-Net, Italy

Technical Program Committee

Abdur Rahim Biswas   Create-Net, Italy
Alban Duverdier   Centre National D'Etudes Spatiales (CNES),
                                 France
Andrea Capitanio   Dinah Consulting, Mestre Venezia, Italy
Maria Angeles Vazquez Castro Universitat Autonoma de Barcelona, Spain
Antonio Iera   University "Mediterranea" of Reggio Calabria,
                                 Italy
Alessandro Vanelli-Coralli   University of Bologna, Italy
Sattar B. Sadkhan   University of Babylon, Iraq
Marc Emmelmann   Technical University of Berlin, Germany
Erina Ferro   ISTI-CNR, Pisa, Italy
Franco Davoli   University of Genoa, Italy
Istvan Frigyes   Budapest University of Technologies, Hungary
Thierry Gayraud   Toulouse University of Science, France
Giovanni Giambene   Universita' degli Studi di Siena, Italy
Gianluca Reali   University of Perugia, Italy
Gianmarco Baldini   European Commission, Joint Research Centre,
                                 Ispra, Varese, Italy
Gonzalo Seco Granados   Universitat Autonoma de Barcelona, Spain
Haitham Cruickshank   Centre for Communication Systems Research,
                                 University of Surrey, UK
Ilias Andrikopoulos   Space Hellas, Greece
Igor Bisio   University of Genoa, Italy

Francisco Javier González
    Castaño   Universidad de Vigo, Spain
Konstantinos Liolis   Space Hellas, Greece
Periklis Chatzimisios   TEI of Thessaloniki, Greece
Petia Todorova   Fraunhofer-FOKUS, Germany
Francesco Potortì   ISTI-CNR, Pisa, Italy
Rafael Asorey Cacheda   Universidad de Vigo, Spain
Sandro Scalise   DLR (German Aerospace Center), Germany
Tarik Taleb   Tohoku University, Japan
Athanasios Panagopoulos   National Technical University of Athens,
                                        Greece
Tomaso de Cola   DLR (German Aerospace Center), Germany
Ruhai Wang   Lamar University, USA
Paolo Villoresi   University of Padova, Italy
Toyoshima, Morio   NICT, Japan
Takaya Yamazat   Nagoya University, Japan

Table of Contents

Analysing the Orbital Movement and Trajectory of LEO (Low Earth Orbit) Satellite Relative to Earth Rotation[*]

Nafeesa Bohra[1], Hermann De Meer[1], and Aftab. A. Memon[2]

[1] Chair of Computer Networks and Computer Communications,
Faculty of Informatics and Mathematics, ITZ/IH,
University of Passau, Innstr. 43, D - 94032, Passau, Germany
{bohra,demeer}@fmi.uni-passau.de
[2] Chair, Department of Telecommunication Engineering,
Mehran University of Engineering & Technology, Jamshoro, Pakistan
{aftab.memon@muet.edu.pk}

Abstract. Next generation of wireless Internet scenarios include LEOs (Low Earth Orbit Satellites). Lower altitudes of LEO constellations could allow global coverage while offering: low end-to-end propagation delay, low power consumption, and effective frequency usage both for the users and the satellite network. LEOs rotate asynchronously to the earth rotation. Fast movement of LEOs makes it necessary to include efficient mobility management. In past few years mobility patterns have been proposed by considering the full earth coverage constellation whereby, the rotation of earth was often assumed too negligible to be taken into account. The prime objective of this study is to provide facts and figures that show LEOs traverse relative to the rotation of earth. In order to analyse the orbital movement and trajectory of LEOs relative to earth rotation mathematical analysis have been done and justification have been made through equations.

Keywords: Orbital movement, Trajectory, LEOs.

1 Introduction

With the advancement of communication technology in general and wireless communication in particular, the use of small size and hand held devices such as laptops, PDAs (Personal Digital Assistance) etc. is increasing day by day. The use of such devices has created a challenging task for researchers in order to provide scalable communication networks. LEO networks are gaining popularity because of the advantage that satellite constellation covering most of the surface of earth could provide connectivity in isolated areas such as rural or transit ways. The advantage of using LEOs lie in their low end-to-end propagation delay, and low power consumption while effectively re-uses the available bandwidth. As far as civil, military, and personal global communication is concerned, LEO satellites will play an

---

[*] This work was partially funded by the EuroNF (European Network of the Future), NoE, FP7 (ICT – 2007 - 1).

K. Sithamparanathan (Ed.): Psats 2009, LNICST 15, pp. 1–11, 2009.
© ICST Institute for Computer Sciences, Social-Informatics and Telecommunications Engineering 2009

important role in next generation of Internet. Integrating LEO satellite in the Internet [[Sun 05], [Woo 03]] remains closely dependable on an effective mobility management which accommodates short connectivity windows with any single point on earth due to satellite's movement. The dynamic nature of satellite (high rotational speed) has been dealt with by increasing the number of satellites in a constellation in order to provide coverage across the globe.

A LEO satellite network [[Woo 03], [UAYY 99]] comprises a constellation of satellites circling at near polar inclination (their angle of inclination lies between the equatorial plane and the satellite orbital plane where as a true polar orbit has an inclination of $90°$) are launched at an altitude between $500 - 1500$ (Km). According to [[Sun 05], [Yeo 03]] Kepler's law of planetary motion, a satellite's orbit is an ellipse and the body it orbits is at one focus. The speed of LEO satellite increases with decreasing altitude (height of the satellite) and the dynamic nature [[AUB 99], [MRER 91]] makes the problem concerning mobility more challenging. Mobility models such as ATCR (Adaptive Time-Based Channel Reservation Algorithm), TCRA (Time-Based Channel Reservation Algorithm), GH (Guaranteed Handover) [[BBGP 03], [BGP 02], [MRRFG 98]] have been proposed for LEO satellites in past few years. However, in all the said strategies, the movement of earth and that of user is being neglected because of the fact that LEOs traverse with high speed relative to the rotation of earth and that of user.

Mobility models presented by [[Yeo 03], [NOT 02]] are designed by taken into consideration the rotation of earth. First model [NOT 02] is designed by taken into consideration that the earth is rotating with a constant linear speed of 1670 (Km/hr), which is not true. Fact is that the rotational speed of earth decreases with cosine of the latitude. The speed 1670 (Km/hr) is the maximum rotational speed of earth at the equator ($0°$ latitude). Second model [Yeo 03] is proposed by taken into consideration that the earth is rotating at an angle of $23.5°$ which is also not true because $23.5°$ is an axial tilt which is constant and is responsible for the change of seasons through out the year.

The earth is tilted at $23.5°$ after every 3 months and that is why the change in seasons occurs. This axial tilt has nothing to do with the orbital movement of LEOs as such satellites are not responsible for bringing change in season. However, the rotational speed of earth decreases with increasing latitude which affects both the orbital movement and trajectory of LEO satellites.

The aim of this study is to analyse mathematically the orbital movement and trajectory of LEOs relative to the rotation of earth. The study is based [[Heindl 05], [FRGT 98], [WJLB 95], [UWE]] upon the orbital parameters of IRIDIUM and UWE–1 because of the fact that both are launched at an altitude between $700 - 800$ (Km) with minimum angle of elevation α_{min} of $10°$ and an inclination angle of $86.4°$ and $98.19 0°$ respectively as shown in Table 1. An inclination angle [Sun 05] measured in degrees, is an angle which determines how much a satellite's orbit is tilted with respect to the equatorial plane of earth. However, in order to provide coverage to the users sufficiently high angle of elevation α of a satellite is required. An angle of elevation α in degrees is an angle between the centre of satellite beam and the surface of earth.

> Elevation angle affects satellite's coverage area (area on the earth's surface where satellite is seen). Ideally an elevation angle of $0°$ is required so that the transmission beam reaches the horizon visible to the satellite in all directions.
> However, because of the environmental factors like: objects blocking the transmission, atmospheric attenuation, and earth's electrical background noise there is a minimum elevation angle α min of earth stations.
> Minimum angle of elevation α min in degrees is required to communicate with the satellite.

Table 1. Orbital Parameters

Attributes	IRIDIUM Constellation	UWE – 1 (Single satellite)
No. of satellites	66	1
No. of orbital planes	6	1
Satellites per plane	11	1
Altitude (Km)	780	800
Inclination (degrees)	86.4°	98.190°
Min. angle of elevation α min (degrees)	10°	10°
Orbital period T_{sat} (min)	Approx.102 min	Approx.102 min

CubeSat [UWE] UWE–1 was built by the engineers at University of Wuerzburg, Germany and is launched in October 2005. The study of orbital movement of LEOs relative to earth's rotation is based upon realistic and accurate facts.

The rest of the paper is organised as follows. Section II gives the mathematical analysis of the rotation of earth and depending upon that analysis the orbital movement and trajectory of LEO satellite has been studied in section III. Conclusion and future work is given in section IV.

2 Orbital Rotation of Earth

LEOs rotate around their orbital plane faster than the rotation of earth and hence continuously circulate around the surface of earth. As is described in [Sun 05] a satellite orbit plane and a point on the orbit can define the satellite trajectory. Satellite orbits lie in planes and hence bisect the orbiting body because of the fact that earth rotates continuously. It can be said that if earth is not rotating continuously then the orbiting satellite would have passed over the same point on earth crossing the equator repeatedly at the same longitude. It is therefore, very important to consider the rotation of earth while designing the mobility model of LEOs.

Continuous rotation of earth has been effective both upon the movement and trajectory of LEOs and in order to determine the length of LEO satellite's orbit around the earth it is necessary to calculate earth's circumference and how it rotates throughout the day. Above mentioned factors must be kept in consideration when orbital movement of LEO satellite is taken into account.

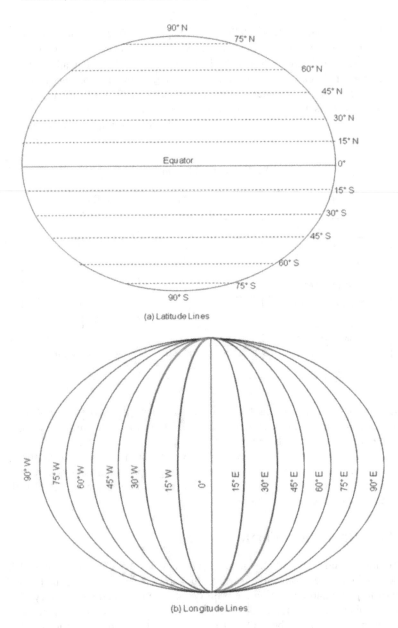

Fig. 1. (a) Latitude lines **(b)** Longitude lines

Consider Fig.1 which shows latitude and longitude lines. From Fig.1 (a), moving from 0° latitude (equator) towards 90° (North or South pole) then the circumference of circle defined by that latitude line will decrease in direct proportion to the cosine of the angle of latitude or simply it can be said that the circumference of earth decreases with increasing latitude. Hence, it is quite obvious to calculate the maximum circumference at equator where latitude is $0°$.

$$C = 2\pi R_E * (Cos\phi) \qquad (1)$$

Where C is the circumference of earth, R_E is the mean radius of earth (6378Km) and ϕ is the latitude in degrees ($0°$ at the equator) and $Cos\phi = Cos0° = 1$. From Eq. (1) maximum value of the earth's circumference C at equator would be $40.075\ 9$(Km). Angular speed of earth $\omega_{earth} = 2\pi f$ or $\omega_{earth} = 2\pi / T$ as $T = 1/f$ is constant irrespective of the latitude, where $T = T_{earth}$ (earth's orbital period $= 24$hr). The angular speed $\omega_{earth} = 2\pi / T_{earth}$ or $360°/24$ (hr) $= 360°/ (24 * 60)$ (min) $= 0.25$ (deg/min). It is concluded that earth rotate $1°$ in 4 minutes. Linear velocity of earth $v_{earth} = d/t$ where $d = C$ (circumference of earth) and $t = T_{earth}$ is 1669.75 (Km /hr) at the equator. Also, v_{earth} decreases with cosine of the latitude which gives the rotational speed $v_{rotation}$ of earth as is calculated in Eq. (2)

$$v_{rotation} = v_{earth} * Cos\phi \qquad (2)$$

$If \phi = 10°$, then

$$v_{rotation} = 1669.75 * Cos10° = 1644.38(Km/hr)$$

From the above analysis it is clear that the rotational speed of earth decreases with increasing latitude and also earth rotate $1°$ in 4 minutes, therefore the mobility models proposed in [[Yeo 03], [NOT 02]] are not practical.

Keeping in view the above mentioned facts how the earth rotates throughout the day, next section will analyse the orbital movement and trajectory of LEOs relative to earth rotation.

3 Orbital Movement and Trajectory of LEOs Relative to Earth Rotation

A LEO network comprises a constellation of satellites such as [FRGT 98] IRIDIUM or for example; a single satellite such as [UWE] UWE–1, launched at an altitude between $700 – 800$ (Km) and are near polar orbiting satellites. One of the advantages [Wikipedia.org1] [daviddarling.info] of these satellites is that they move in sun–synchronous orbits which combine altitude and inclination and are typically low earth orbits with the range of altitudes mentioned above and period approximately equal to 102 (min) as given in Table 1. Sun-synchronous orbit [crisp.edu.sg] is a near polar orbit and the sun–synchronous movement of the satellite causes it to pass through the equator and each degree of latitude exactly the same local solar time every day and hence passes overhead at the same solar time throughout the year. Therefore, in order to collect regular data, for example, weather forecast, remote sensing, etc. LEOs can be effectively used. Except for the seasonal variation (which takes place due to an axial tilt of $23.5°$ after every 3 months) same illumination conditions can be achieved for the images of a given location taken by the satellite and comparisons can easily be made.

Main purpose of this study is to mathematically analyse the orbital movement and trajectory of a LEO satellite relative to the rotation of earth with the help of orbital parameters of [[FRGT 98], [UWE]] IRRIDIUM and UWE–1. The orbital period [[Heindl 05], [FRGT 98], [WJLB 95]] T_{sat} as given in Table 1 for IRRIDIUM and UWE–1 is approximately 102 (min) and earth rotates 0.25 (deg/min) hence, earth will be rotated at an angle of $25.5°$ ($0.25 * 102$) when LEO satellite completes one orbital rotation.

$$\lambda_{NR} \text{ (degrees longitude/rotation)} = 0.25 * T_{sat} \tag{3}$$

$$0.25° * 102 = 25.5 \text{ (degrees longitude /rotation)}.$$

Consider Table 2 which summarizes the values for λ_{NR} after every T_{sat} for few N_R (number of rotations). It can be seen from Table 2 that if LEO satellite starts when $\lambda_{NR} = 0°$ longitude (west) with $T_{sat} = 00 : 00$ (min) then it will again cross the equator after 51 (min) on one side of the earth and 102 (min) on the other side of earth at $25.5°$ longitude (west). For the next rotation the equator crossing on the same side will take place again after 102 (min) at $51°(25.5° + 25.5°)$ west longitude. Longitude lines are shown in Fig. 1(b).

It can be said that with an orbital period of 102 (min) the longitudinal increment is 25.5 degrees per rotation. Therefore, in order to cover the whole day (24hrs) or ($24 * 60 = 1440$min) the satellite will need $T_{earth} / T_{sat} = 1440/102 = 14.117$ rotations per day. It is concluded that at the end of the day the satellite will start its 15th rotation and has completed 14 rotations across the globe and at the same time the earth will also complete its rotation of $360°$.

From Table 2 and from the discussion given in Section II and Section III respectively, it is concluded that both the earth and the satellite are simultaneously

Table 2. Satellite crossing at the equator

N_R = No. of Rotation	T_{sat}(min) $= 102$(min)	λ_{NR}($0.25 * 102 = 25.5$) degrees longitude/rotation after every T_{sat})
$N_R = 0$	$T_o = 00 : 00$	$\lambda_o = 0°$
$N_R = 1$	$T_1 = T_o + T_{sat}$	$\lambda_1 = \lambda_o + 25.5°$
$N_R = 2$	$T_2 = T_1 + T_{sat}$	$\lambda_2 = \lambda_1 + 25.5°$
$N_R = 3$	$T_3 = T_2 + T_{sat}$	$\lambda_3 = \lambda_2 + 25.5°$
$N_R = n$ rotations, $n = 0,1,2,- - -$	$T_n = n * T_{sat}$, $n = 0,1,2,- - -$	$\lambda_n = n * 25.5°$ $n = 0,1,2,- - -$

changing their trajectories with the passage of time. Table 2 gives the new value after every rotation, whereas our aim is to find out the exact trajectory of the satellite relative to earth rotation which depends upon:

> D_{nad} (Nadir distance) is the distance in Km travelled by the nadir point on the surface of earth during one rotation. The Nadir point is a point [[HK 99], [wikipedia.org2]] on the surface of the earth directly between the satellite and the geo – centre (centre of earth), and is also referred as sub-satellite point, as shown in Fig. 2.

> t_u the time during which the signal is available to the users (time usable by the users).

> D_{rec} distance in Km from user's location to the points on earth over which the satellite will come into LOS (line of sight) and leave i.e. diameter of reception area or in other words coverage area of satellite as shown in Fig.3.

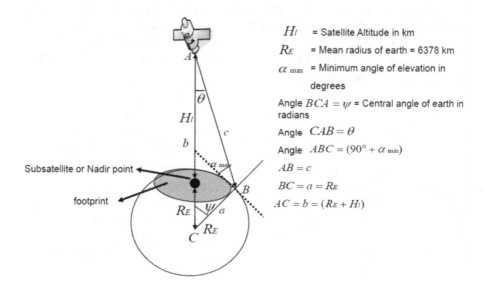

Fig. 2. Central angle of Earth

D_{nad} can be calculated with the help of the linear velocity V_{nad} of the nadir point by which the satellite traverses on the surface of earth. $V_{nad} = V_{sat}$ for LEO satellites [FRGT 98] relative to earth is given by Eq. (4) where R_g is GEO satellite orbit radius $(R_E + H_g)$, R_l is LEO satellite orbit radius $(R_E + H_l)$, H_g is altitude of GEO satellite, and H_l is altitude of LEO satellite respectively.

$$V_{nad} = \omega_{earth} * (\sqrt[3]{R_g} / \sqrt{R_l}) \qquad (4)$$

D_{nad} is calculated in Eq.(5).

$$V_{nad} = D_{nad} / T_{sat}$$

$$D_{nad} = V_{nad} * T_{sat} \tag{5}$$

A LEO satellite completes at least 14.117 rotations per day; hence, total distance covered by the satellite D_{cov} during 24 (hr) or 1440 (min) is given by Eq. (6).

$$D_{cov} = D_{nad} * \text{No. of rotations per day} \tag{6}$$

D_{rec} is calculated using Fig.3. Consider Fig.3 where the inner circle represents the surface of earth while the outer circle represents a single satellite orbiting around the earth. The point L on the inner circle (earth surface) represent the user's location while a straight line through point L represents the horizon as it can be seen from point L (user's location). If it is assumed that users will only receive a signal when the satellite passes overhead, then mark two points A and B respectively where the horizon line intersects the outer circle (satellite orbit). Point A represents the point from where the satellite appears to be in LOS of the user whereas point B represents the point where the satellite appears out of LOS of the user. In the inner circle D_{rec} represents the diameter of reception area (coverage area of satellite) while R_{rec} is the radius of reception area.

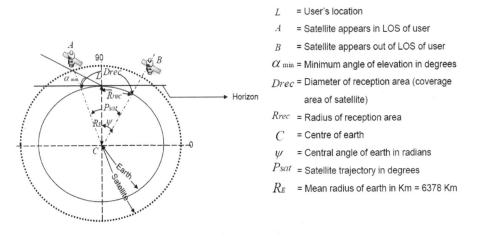

L	= User's location
A	= Satellite appears in LOS of user
B	= Satellite appears out of LOS of user
α_{min}	= Minimum angle of elevation in degrees
D_{rec}	= Diameter of reception area (coverage area of satellite)
R_{rec}	= Radius of reception area
C	= Centre of earth
ψ	= Central angle of earth in radians
P_{sat}	= Satellite trajectory in degrees
R_E	= Mean radius of earth in Km = 6378 Km

Fig. 3. Single satellite orbiting earth

We are interested in calculating the maximum distance from our location (point L) at which the satellite signal is expected to be received by the users. D_{rec} is actually the size of the instantaneous coverage of satellite as described in [MRER 91] and is given by Eq. (7).

$$D_{rec} = 2R_E \psi \tag{7}$$

ψ as is described in [[WJBL 95], [MRER 91]] is the central angle of earth in radians as shown in Fig.2 and is calculated by Eq. (8), which depends upon H_l the altitude of LEOs in Km, α_{min} the minimum angle of elevation in degrees and R_E the mean radius of earth in Km.

$$\psi = InvCos\ [R_E * Cos\,\alpha_{min}/(R_E + R_l)] - \alpha_{min} \tag{8}$$

The radius of reception area R_{rec} becomes:

$$R_{rec} = D_{rec}/2 = R_E\psi \tag{9}$$

The distance D_{rec} is an important factor as it defines the geographical boundaries where a communication system can be used and is also helpful in determining the time interval during which the satellite signal is usable to the user. Exact time during which the satellite signal is usable to the user is calculated from Eq. (10).

$$D_{nad}/T_{sat} = D_{rec}/t_u \tag{10}$$

Where t_u is the time during which the signal is usable to user in minutes and is given by Eq. (11).

$$t_u = (T_{sat} * D_{rec})/D_{nad} \tag{11}$$

From Eq. (11) it is concluded that the satellite will be out of sight of the user after t_u (min). t_u is an important factor as it helps in calculating the trajectory of the satellite relative to earth rotation in terms of degree. The trajectory of satellite P_{sat} can be obtained as a product of ω_{sat} angular speed of satellite and t_u.

$$P_{sat} = \omega_{sat} * t_u \tag{12}$$

Where $\omega_{sat} = 2\pi/T_{sat} = 360°/T_{sat}$

As mentioned in section II that the earth rotate 1° in 4 minutes and the earth will also be at a new position after every t_u. The trajectory of earth P_{earth} is calculated in Eq. (13).

$$P_{earth} = t_u * (1°/4min) \tag{13}$$

t_u as calculated in Eq. (11) gives the time during which a single satellite for example, [UWE] UWE–1 is visible to the user. From the above discussion it is concluded that once the satellite will be out of sight from the 1st location it will be visible at another location on the surface of earth. In order to provide continuous coverage to the users a constellation of satellite such as [FRGT 98] IRIDIUM is required.

From Eq. (12) and Eq. (13) it is proved that both earth and satellite are changing their trajectories with the passage of time and hence, the models presented in [[Yeo 03], [NOT 02]] are not justified. In this study the prime objective is to calculate the trajectory of a satellite and how a satellite moves with respect to the rotation of earth. The issue how handover takes place if the rotation of earth is not neglected as is done in most of the available models is left as future work.

4 Conclusion

After this study it is concluded that it is unjustified to consider that the earth is rotating with a constant linear speed of 1670 (Km/hr) as is considered in Nguyen et al's model because this means that the satellite will cross the equator again and again at the same longitude and hence not able to provide global coverage. Also, it is not reasonable to consider that the earth is rotating at an angle of 23.5°, which actually is an axial tilt (earth is tilted at this angle after every 3 months), it would again mean that the satellite would not be able to complete its rotation of 360° during the orbital period of 102 (min) and ultimately not able to move around the surface of earth when the day is finished. Therefore, no global coverage is achieved. From Eq. (12) and Eq. (13) it is also concluded that the trajectories of satellite and that of earth changes continuously with the passage of time. The prime objective of this study is to provide facts and figures that show LEOs traverse relative to the rotation of earth. How handover takes place when a constellation of satellite is taken into consideration by taken into account the rotation of earth is left as future work.

References

[AUB 99]   Akylidiz, I.F., Uzunalioglu, H., Bender, M.D.: Handover Management in Low Earth Orbit (LEO) Satellite Networks. Mobile Networks and Application 4(4), 301–310 (1999)

[BBGP 03]   Boukhatem, L., Beylot, A.L., Gaiti, D., Pujolle, G.: TCRP: A Time-Based Channel Reservation Schemes for Handover Requests in LEO Satellite Systems. Int. J. of Satellite Communications and Networking 21(3), 227–240 (2003)

[BGP 02]   Boukhatem, L., Gaiti, D., Pujolle, G.: Resource Reservation Schemes for Handover Issue in LEO Satellite Systems. In: 5th Int. Symposium on Wireless Personal Multimedia Communication, October 2002, vol. 3, pp. 1217–1221 (2002)

[crisp.edu.sg]   http://www.crisp.nus.edu.sg/~research/tutorial/spacebrn.htm

[daviddarling.info] http://www.daviddarling.info/encyclopedia/S/sun-synchronous_orbit.html

[FRGT 98]   Fossa, C.E., Raines, R.A., Gunsch, G.H., Temple, M.A.: An Overview of the Iridium® Low Earth Orbit (LEO) Satellite. In: Proc. of IEEE National Aerospace and Electronics Conference, NAECON 1998, pp. 152–159. Dayton, U.S.A (1998)

[Heindl 05]   Heindl, M.: Quality of Service for Satellite Links. Bachelor Thesis. University of Passau (November 2005)

[HK 99]   Henderson, T.R., Katz, R.H.: Network Simulation for LEO Satellite Networks. AIAA (American Institute of Aeronautics and Astronautics) (1999)

[MRER 91]   Maral, G., De Ridder, J.J., Evans, G.G., Richharia, M.: Low Earth Orbit Satellite System for Communications. Int. J. Satellite Communication 9, 209–225 (1991)

[MRRFG 98]   Maral, G., Restrepo, J., Del Re, E., Fantacci, R., Giambene, G.: Performance Analysis for a Guaranteed Handover Service in an LEO Constellation with a Satellite fixed Cell System. IEEE Transactions on Vehicular Technology 47(4), 1200–1214 (1998)

[NOT 02]   Nguyen, H.N., Olariu, S., Todorova, P.: A Novel Mobility Model and Resource Reservation Strategy for Multimedia LEO Satellite Networks. In: Wireless Communications and Networking Conference (WCNC 2002), March 2002, vol. 2, pp. 832–836 (2002)

[RFG 94]   Del Re, E., Fantacci, R., Giambene, G.: Performance Analysis of Dynamic Channel Allocation Technique for Satellite Mobile Cellular Networks. IEEE J. on Selected Area in Communication 12(1), 25–32 (1994)

[RFG 95]   del Re, E., fantacci, R., Giambene, G.: Efficient Dynamic Channel Allocation Techniques with Handover Queuing for Mobile Satellite Networks. IEEE J. on Selected Area in Communications 13(2), 397–405 (1995)

[SUN 05]   Sun, Z.: Satellite Networking, Principles and Protocols. John Wiley and Sons, Chichester (2005)

[UAYY 99]   Uzunalioglu, H., Akyildiz, I.F., Yesha, Y., Yen, W.: Footprint Handover Rerouting Protocol for Low Earth Orbit Satellite Networks. Wireless Network 5(5), 327–337 (1999)

[UWE]   UWE-1, http://www7.informatik.uni-Wuerzburg.de/cubeset/index

[WJBL 95]   Werner, M., Jahn, A., Lutz, E., Bottcher, A.: Analysis of System Parameters for LEO/ICO Satellite Communication Networks. IEEE J. on selected Area in Communication 13(2), 371–381 (1995)

[Wikipedia.org1] http://en.wikipedia.org/wiki/Sun-synchronous

[Wikipedia.org2] http://en.wikipedia.org/wiki/Nadir

[Woo 03]   Wood, L.: Satellite Communication Networks. In: Internetworking and Computing over Satellite Networks, ch. 2, March 2003, pp. 13–34 (2003)

[Yeo 03]   Yeo, B.S.: An Analysis of the Impact of Earth Rotation on LEO Satellite Mobility Model. In: The 57th IEEE Semi-annual Vehicular Technology Conference, April 2003, vol. 2, pp. 1376–1380 (2003)

A Cross-Layer PEP for DVB-RCS Networks

Giovanni Giambene and Snezana Hadzic

CNIT - University of Siena, Via Roma, 56, I-53100 Siena, Italy
giambene@unisi.it

Abstract. The aim of this paper is to consider the problems of TCP performance in broadband GEO satellite networks and to propose a cross-layer approach for a transport-layer PEP that makes spoofing actions on ACKs to modify them in case the satellite network is congested. This approach is investigated here from the signaling standpoint with a special attention to the BSM reference model and considering a specific GEO satellite network architecture based on the DVB-S2/-RCS standards. The proposed PEP can prevent congestion in the satellite network, thus allowing a better TCP performance. This work has been carried out within the framework of the EU SatNEx II FP6 Network of Excellence.

Keywords: Satellite Networks, BSM, DVB-RCS, TCP, PEP.

1 Introduction

The ETSI working group *Broadband Satellite Multimedia* (BSM) has defined [1] a reference architecture where the protocol stack is divided into two main blocks connected by the *Satellite Independent-Service Access Point* (SI-SAP): the upper part of protocols is characteristic of the Internet and independent of the satellite implementation (i.e., IP-based protocol suite), while the lower part depends on the satellite system technology. Primitives are used to exchange signaling on the control plane across SI-SAP between these two blocks of protocol layers. The BSM standard envisages a framework for *Quality of Service* (QoS) support, allowing a mapping between layer 3 traffic classes and layer 2 technology-dependent allocation methods.

DVB-S2 is a second-generation standard for forward link communications in broadband satellite networks for broadcast, multicast, and interactive services [2]. Note that 28 *Modulation and Coding* (ModCod) combinations are possible in the standard. The transmission is typically organized in blocks of 25 MHz in Ku or Ka bands. *Adaptive Coding and Modulation* (ACM) is used for interactive traffic and permits to change dynamically the ModCod level, depending on channel conditions by means of E_b/N_0 ModCod thresholds determined to guarantee *Frame Error Rate* (FER) below 10^{-7} in the *Additive White Gaussian Noise* (AWGN) channel case (*Quasi Error-Free*, QEF, operation). The sender dynamically acquires information on the receiver channel conditions by means of a return link. The DVB-RCS specifications have been introduced to allow a return path for satellite networks based on DVB-S/-S2 [3]. The return channel

K. Sithamparanathan (Ed.): Psats 2009, LNICST 15, pp. 12–19, 2009.

can dynamically assign its time-frequency resources (*Multi-Frequency - Time Division Multiple Access*, MF-TDMA, air interface) to the terminals. SatLab recommendations have defined QoS mechanisms for DVB-S2/-RCS on the basis of the BSM framework [4]. A new specification has been recently released to support mobile users. This specification (called DVB-RCS+M) has been issued by the DVB organization in its Blue Book [5]. Some basic features of DVB-RCS+M are the adoption of spread spectrum techniques, the support of different handover scenarios, the adoption of shadow/fading-resilient techniques (Link Layer FEC), and the ACM support also in the return link.

At present, the air interface is based on the separate design of protocols at distinct OSI layers (PHY, MAC, Network, Transport, Application), thus reducing the complexity and allowing the interoperability among equipments of different manufacturers. However, due to the dynamic nature of the radio channel, there exists a tight interdependence between layers in satellite systems that should be better exploited than allowed by the classical OSI stack based on the layer separation principle. This is evident especially in the presence of ACM-based air interfaces, such as DVB-S2 or DVB-RCS+M. As an example, the higher the ModCod is, the greater the available bandwidth, but also the higher the packet error rate for a given channel condition [6]. These two aspects have opposite impacts on TCP goodput, as expressed by the well known *square-root formula* for the TCP NewReno version [7]. Hence, a suitable tradeoff should be found for ModCod selection (i.e., ModCod threshold values in terms of E_b/N_0) depending on channel characteristics and TCP behavior.

Current research interest in wireless as well as in satellite communications is on protocol architectures where the reference OSI stack is enriched with interactions between protocols even at non-adjacent layers, according to a *cross-layer design* [8]. One interesting aspect of cross-layering is the need to allow the direct exchange of control information (signaling) even among non-adjacent layers [9]. In general, different techniques could be used to support the exchange of signaling information. In particular, two relevant and complementary methods are [6],[9]:

- *In-band signaling* with the use of enriched packet headers to notify internal state variables to either other layers within a given host (internal cross-layering) or in a peer-to-peer case with another host or gateway (external cross-layering). This method needs the redefinition of packets headers (e.g., use of spare bits). This method is for signaling going in the same direction of related data.
- *Out-of-band signaling* via the control plane, that is the use of new primitives and suitable SAPs to allow the dialogue between protocol layers.

This paper deals with the study of *Performance Enhancing Proxy* (PEP) techniques [10] and the possibility to apply cross-layer methods to improve transport layer performance for BSM-compliant DVB-S2/-RCS networks. This work derives from a cooperation between the SatNEx II ja2230 activity (entitled "Cross-Layer Protocol Design") [11] and the ETSI BSM working group [12].

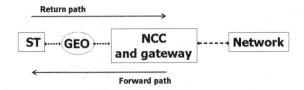

Fig. 1. Reference system architecture

2   BSM-Compliant Reference Scenario

The interest is here for a scenario where DVB-S2 is used for the forward channel with ModCod adaptation and DVB-RCS is used for the return channel with DAMA (*Dynamic Assignment Multiple Access*) controlled by the *Network Control Center* (NCC). The envisaged satellite is of the GEO type and the network is IP-based. We make the assumption that in the satellite network NCC, gateway, and feeder are co-located; the gateway implements a transport-layer PEP. The NCC manages resource allocation in the satellite network, but it is also the network element through which the traffic is exchanged with the Internet. The building blocks of our satellite network scenario are described in Figure 1.

The protocol stack is compliant with the BSM standard at both the *Satellite Terminal* (ST) and the NCC/gateway. Moreover, it is assumed that one layer is in charge of controlling the cross-layer signaling exchange with *primitives*; in our study this is the case of the MAC layer (MAC-centric approach). These new interactions can be used at the ST and/or at the NCC/gateway.

Several layer 2 queues are needed to support different resource allocation methods. The definition of these queues is technology-dependent. In the DVB-RCS case, Satlab work can be considered for the definition of layer 2 allocation techniques with QoS support [4]. The SI-SAP interface allows a general framework for mapping L3 queues on those at MAC layer. This is obtained by means of QIDs (*Queue Identifiers*), abstract queues that represent layer 2 queues in a general way [13].

Cross-layer techniques could be supported by BSM primitives (control plane) used through SI-SAP between MAC and L3([1]). These primitives concern the interactions between the "L3 queue manager" (it manages the queues that are present at the IP level; its functions depend on the IP QoS scheme adopted, that is DiffServ or IntServ) and the layer 2 *Satellite Terminal QID Resource Manager* (STQRM; its functions are: association of QIDs to satellite-dependent queues, translating QIDSPEC into values that are suitable to request satellite-dependent resources, control of resource allocation, translation of primitives arriving at the SI-SAP into lower layer primitives and vice versa) [14]. The simplified layer 2 and 3 protocol architecture of the BSM model is shown in Figure 2.

---

[1] Even if we consider here adjacent layers, we still have cross-layer interactions in the wide sense that primitives allow the exchange of internal state variables that otherwise would only be used by the related layer.

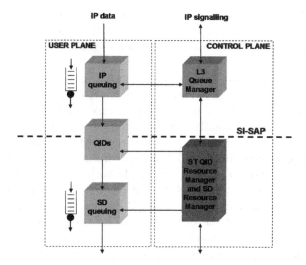

Fig. 2. L3 queuing, QID mapping, and resource management functions at layer 2 according to the BSM model

Cross-layer interactions require an innovative design of the air interface with new primitives among layers. BSM primitives only permit interactions between layer 3 and layer 2 [14]. There is, therefore, the need to include mechanisms to allow the exchange of signaling also among non-adjacent layers. One possibility could be to define some broadcast 'primitives' on the control plane (in upward and downward direction on a 'bus' shared by all the layers, a sort of vertical 'pipe') delivering messages and contents that each layer could simultaneously acquire and use for its purposes. The following study focuses on adopting new combined approaches like PEP and cross-layer design in order to improve the behavior of TCP in DVB-S2/-RCS satellite networks compliant with the BSM model.

3   PEP-Spoofer with Cross-Layer Signalling

Due to the peculiarities of the architecture in Figure 1, congestion control in the satellite network does not need a 'black box' approach, because the bottleneck is the satellite link and the NCC/gateway can have a direct control on it via the resource allocation decided at layer 2. This very special situation can allow the NCC to anticipate congestion events that otherwise could cause packet losses with a possible drop of the TCP congestion window. These additional transport layer functionalities for the NCC require it to operate as a PEP using cross-layer information exchanged with layer 2. Our interest is here for the return link: STs are servers that send TCP flows towards the network through the NCC/gateway. In this study, a DVB-RCS satellite network is considered where the NCC dynamically assigns radio resources to STs for FTP transmissions through a GEO bent-pipe satellite. We adopt a generic DAMA scheme, controlled by the NCC, that allocates resources on a super-frame basis (MF-TDMA air interface). The proposed cross-layer method is described below (see Figure 3):

1. In the ST, the TCP internal state information (i.e., cwnd and TCP phase, that for the classical TCP could be Slow Start or Congestion Avoidance) is propagated from layer 4 to MAC by means of either suitably enriched headers or a periodic primitive reporting about the state of the transport layer protocol (such primitive, not concerned with the BSM work, should be synchronized with the MF-TDMA super-frame structure and the related DAMA resource request made at layer 2). In both cases, a modification to the DVB-RCS standard would be needed. At layer 2, a DAMA capacity request is sent for next super-frame to the NCC on the basis of the current layer 2 buffer occupancy and the prospected TCP injection of data in the next super-frame. Since the allocation of resources arrives at the ST (at least) after a round trip propagation delay from the request, the request must be done considering a forecast on the packets arrived in the meantime; hence, the capacity request has to be based on the expected TCP cwnd increment in the prospected allocation time. The DAMA request to the NCC needs also to convey the cwnd value of TCP and a layer 3 buffer congestion indication for the ST (a threshold scheme is considered here, where the threshold value should be suitably optimized depending on system characteristics).

2. The NCC receives the incoming DAMA requests, assigns the available resources in the super-frame and notifies the allocation through the *Terminal Burst Time Plan* (TBTP) broadcast message. The NCC may reduce the amount of resources assigned to an ST in a super-frame, if the resources the ST requested are not available; then, the NCC defines at MAC layer a corresponding limit, cwnd*, to the congestion window value (cwnd* < cwnd) for the ST. If the ST buffer is congested (threshold method), the cwnd* value is provided back to the transport layer of the ST with external cross-layer signaling, as detailed at the following point #3. The ST cwnd value is thus blocked to the cwnd* one[2]. This procedure is detailed in Figure 4.

3. The NCC at transport layer is a gateway towards the network and operates as a PEP in the forward path where the ACKs of the TCP flow under consideration are intercepted according to a spoofing action. If the cwnd* value is set for a given ST, such value is included in a suitable field of a transport-layer modified ACK*. Moreover, a flag in the ACK* notifies the ST if the cwnd* option is active. A suitably-modified TCP version running on the ST (sender) should be able to manage the modified ACK* with cwnd*

---

[2] This mechanism to control congestion is effective when there is very low FER (like QEF condition that requires $FER < 10^{-7}$ for fixed users) so that TCP goodput is only affected by timeouts caused by buffer overflows. However, this mechanism could be also useful when there is a higher PER (like in DVB-RCS+M for mobile users, requiring even $PER < 10^{-3}$), but there are many users that cause layer 2 resource congestion.

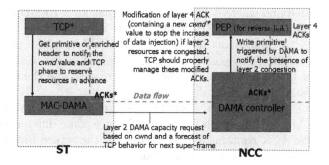

Fig. 3. Case study of cross-layering with in-band and out-of-band signaling. Cross-layer interactions are present at both ST and NCC.

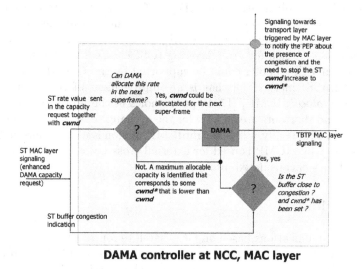

DAMA controller at NCC, MAC layer

Fig. 4. DAMA controller at the NCC with cross-layer functionality (MAC-centric approach)

so that TCP can set the current cwnd to the cwnd* value to block the normal cwnd increase (non-transparent PEP approach).

4. If the condition of resource shortage is solved, the cwnd value of the ST can be unlocked with the reception of standard ACKs that are not modified by the NCC/PEP.

In the presence of many STs contending for the use of the satellite bandwidth with DVB-RCS, the DAMA controller has to schedule their service taking into account a fair sharing of resources since STs may experience different channel conditions. The performance evaluation of the above technique is not the subject of this paper, focused on cross-layer signaling for our PEP proposal and the relationship with SI-SAP. The interested reader may refer to [15] where a similar scheme is presented and where it has been shown that for a 10 MB file transfer, the cross-layer approach with PEP-spoofer allows a transfer time reduction of 26% with respect to *Continuous Rate Assignment* (CRA) in the presence of a packet error rate of 2%. This performance enhancement is due to the combined effect of both the traffic prediction for the DAMA request and the PEP-spoofer to control the congestion in the satellite network.

Note that our PEP-spoofer at the NCC makes use of ACK at transport layer, similarly to the M-TCP approach [16], but there are some differences because in our scheme the ACK contains a cwnd* value for the return link flow, while in M-TCP the ACK contains a receiver window value used for the forward link flow. In our scenario, both approaches could be combined.

In this study, the use of modified ACKs is an example of in-band cross-layer signaling. While, the use of primitives on the control plane is an example of out-of-band signaling. Problematic seems the MAC $\rightarrow$ TCP relation at the NCC (upward signaling), since no conventional mechanism is available to convey information from layer 2 to layer 4 in the BSM model. Since layer-by-layer signaling is an inefficient approach for cross-layering (OSI classical method), cross-layer signaling for our PEP-spoofer could be supported by the *Cross-Layer Signaling Shortcuts* (CLASS) method [9] that is an improvement of the *Internet Control Message Protocol* (ICMP) [17] to punch holes in the protocol stack so that local out-of-band shortcuts are created for the exchange of signaling among non-adjacent layers. Practically, a lightweight ICMP version is used for internal cross-layer signaling, while ICMP is used for external cross-layer signaling. An ICMP message is always encapsulated into an IP packet.

4   Conclusions

Broadband communications based on GEO satellite represent an interesting option to connect to the Internet in many areas of the world. The problem is that TCP is penalized by huge propagation delays and packet losses. A way to accelerate TCP is to make use of PEPs in gateways. In this paper, we have studied a type of PEP that operates on the TCP traffic sent by STs through an NCC/gateway that acts as a PEP-spoofer on ACKs flowing in the opposite direction. Our main interest is on the adopted cross-layer signaling and related information exchange among layers. Our integrated PEP proposal is non-transparent and requires the application of new cross-layer signaling at the PEP/NCC/gateway. A further study (based on simulations) is needed to optimize the characteristics of the PEP proposal and the threshold values used to decide the situation of buffer congestion.

Acknowledgments

This paper has been carried out within the framework of the European SatNEx II (contract No. IST-027393) network of excellence, activity ja2230, and under a one-year CNIT research grant received by Snezana Hadzic.

References

1. ETSI, Satellite Earth Stations and Systems (SES), Broad-band Satellite Multimedia, IP over Satellite, ETSI Technical Report, TR 101 985
2. ETSI, Digital Video Broadcasting (DVB); Second Generation Framing Structure, Channel Coding and Modulation Systems for Broadcasting, Interactive Services, News Gathering and other Broadband Satellite Applications (DVB-S2), EN 302 307
3. ETSI, Digital Video Broadcasting (DVB); Interaction Channel for Satellite Distribution Systems, EN 301 790, V1.3.1 (November 2002)
4. SatLab. SatLab System Recommendations v2 QoS, http://satlabs.org/
5. DVB Interaction channel for Satellite Distribution Systems, BlueBook A054r4.1 (January 2009), http://www.dvb.org/technology/standards
6. Giambene, G., Kota, S.: Cross-layer Protocol Optimization for Satellite Communications Networks: A Survey. Int. Journal Sat. Communications and Networking 24, 323–341 (2006)
7. Barakat, C., Altman, E.: Bandwidth Tradeoff between TCP and link-level FEC. Computer Networks 39(2), 133–150 (2002)
8. Giambene, G. (ed.): Resource Management in Satellite Networks: Optimization and Cross-Layer Design. Springer, New York (2007)
9. Wang, Q., Abu-Rgheff, M.-A.: Cross-layer Signalling for Next-Generation Wireless Systems. In: IEEE Wireless Comms. and Networking Conf. 2003, New Orleans, USA, March 16-20 (2003)
10. Ivanovich, M., Bickerdike, P.W., Li, J.C.: On TCP Performance Enhancing Proxies in a Wireless Environment. IEEE Communications Magazine 46(9), 76–83 (2008)
11. SatNEx II EU FP6 Network of Excellence with Web site: http://www.satnex.org; SatNEx II platform for public dissemination: http://wise.cnit.it/
12. Giambene, G.: Cross-layer Report, ETSI BSM document with code BSM#3607, ETSI-Sophia-Antipolis, France (June 2, 2008)
13. ETSI, Satellite Earth Stations and Systems (SES); Broadband Satellite Multimedia; IP Interworking over satellite; Performance, Availability and Quality of Service, TR 102 157 V1.1.1 (July 2003)
14. ETSI, Satellite Earth Stations and Systems (SES); Broadband Satellite. Multimedia (BSM); Interworking with IntServ QoS, TS 102 463
15. Chini, P., Giambene, G., Bartolini, D., Luglio, M., Roseti, C.: Dynamic Resource Allocation based on a TCP-MAC Cross-Layer Approach for DVB-RCS Satellite Networks. Int. Journal Sat. Communications and Networking 24, 367–385 (2006)
16. Brown, K., Singh, S.: M-TCP: TCP for Mobile Cellular Networks. ACM Comp. Commun. Rev. 27(5), 19–43 (1997)
17. Sudame, P., Badrinath, B.R.: On providing support for protocol adaptation in mobile wireless networks. Mobile Networks and Applications 6(1), 43–55 (2001)

Triple Play over Satellite, Ka-Band Making the Difference

Guillaume Benoit, Hector Fenech, and Stefano Pezzana

Eutelsat
70 rue Balard
75502 Paris, France
{gbenoit,hfenech,spezzana}@eutelsat.fr

Abstract. Over the last years a number of operators have been deploying satellite-based consumer internet access services to reduce the digital divide and capture the market of households not covered by ADSL, cable or wireless broadband. These operators are proposing a step change improvement in the economics of consumer service, with lower terminal costs, broadband access with monthly fees comparable to ADSL and an integrated technology simplifying the process of terminal installation, provisioning and management.

Until now, these services have been focused on internet access only. Now, full triple play services over satellite are available.

This article presents Eutelsat's European Ka band strategy for the Tooway[TM] service and its evolution through a dedicated Ka band-exclusive satellite (KA-SAT). It also explains Eutelsat's choice in selecting the Ka band for interactive services, demonstrating the optimal consumer service synergy between existing Ku band and new Ka band services.

Keywords: Broadband internet access, Ka band, triple play, VoIP, IPTV.

1 Introduction

Eutelsat operates 25 satellites in the geostationary arc from 15°W to 70.5°E offering a variety of services from corporate networks to broadcasting (see Fig. 1). The HOT BIRD™ constellation at 13°E constitutes the prime position for DTH (Direct to Home) and cable broadcasting, utilising the full Ku-band spectrum from 10.70 GHz to 12.75 GHz. There are 102 transponders delivering about 1100 TV channels. The HOT BIRD™ service area reaches into some 120 million satellite and cable households.

The original constellation comprised five satellites. Beginning in 2009, it will be made up of three satellites including HOT BIRD™ 6 and the high-capacity HOT BIRD™ 8 and HOT BIRD™ 9 satellites to further improve in-orbit reliability. Video services contribute to approximately three quarters of Eutelsat's revenue.

With DTH and cable broadcasting, the main objective is to cover as many households as possible through a single service area. However, the requirements of broadband access move away from broadcast to unicast as the data accessed on the Internet by a given user is generally intended for that given user at that given instant.

K. Sithamparanathan (Ed.): Psats 2009, LNICST 15, pp. 20–28, 2009.

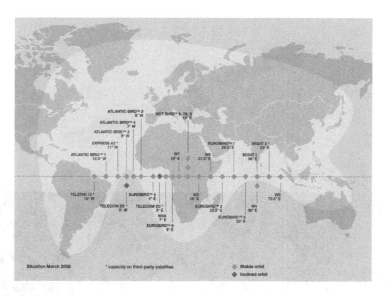

Fig. 1. The Eutelsat satellites on the geostationary arc

The KA-SAT system calls for specific system concepts which are different from those of DTH systems. The main objective is to ensure that the cost for the system capacity permits a competitive consumer interactive service.

2 The KA-SAT Satellite

KA-SAT will be the first European multi-beam satellite to operate exclusively in Ka-band and dedicated to providing broadband and broadcast services in Extended Europe. It will be launched mid-2010 and positioned at 13 degrees East in geostationary orbit (see Fig. 2).

The satellite is being manufactured by EADS-Astrium based on their Spacebus 3000 platform.

KA-SAT will operate simultaneously 82 spotbeams, which makes it the largest multi-beam Ka-band satellite ever ordered worldwide and also offering the largest service area. The satellite will feature a high level of frequency re-use. The spacecraft is equipped with four multi-feeds deployable antennas with enhanced pointing accuracy and a high efficiency repeater. The cells cover Europe and parts of the Middle East and North Africa as shown in Fig. 3. Efficient frequency reuse enables the system to achieve a total capacity that is in excess of 70 Gb/s. The introduction of KA-SAT will triple the total capacity commercialised by Eutelsat.

ViaSat has ordered a similar satellite for North America, from Space Systems Loral based on their L1300 platform. To be launched in 2011, its total capacity is in excess of 100 Gb/s and constitute with KA-SAT the satellites with largest capacity ever built. Together, KA-SAT and ViaSat-1 represent a new class of satellites with the potential to change the way the world views fixed satellite services.

Fig. 2. KA-SAT satellite

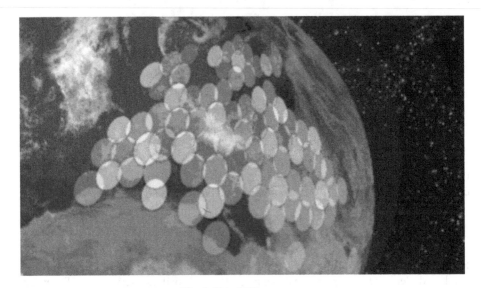

Fig. 3. KA-SAT coverage

KA-SAT will supply Eutelsat with a substantial platform for expansion of its Tooway™ consumer broadband service which was launched in 2007 via Ka-band capacity already available on its HOT BIRD™ 6 satellite and in Ku-band via EUROBIRD™ 3.

3 Why Ka-Band for KA-SAT

Several reasons explain Eutelsat's choice to manufacture a dedicated Ka band satellite for interactive services :

1. There is more exclusive spectrum available at Ka-band. The Exclusive Band in Ku-band is limited to 250 MHz on the uplink and spans from 14.25 GHz to 14.50 GHz while the available spectrum at Ka-band is double that spectrum, i.e. 500 MHz on both uplink (29.5 – 30GHz) and downlink (19.7 – 20.2GHz). The Exclusive Band in Ka-band has a better interference environment and its use is limited to small terminals. The equivalent in

Ku-band is more widely used and interference could be the limiting factor in terms of terminal size for the Return Link.

2. The antenna gain and free space loss are functions of the square of the frequency. Thus assuming that the satellite antenna aperture is limited by the satellite configuration and the launch vehicle fairing and that the terminal aperture is defined by the service, the improvement in the link budget under clear sky conditions is also a function of the square of the frequency inducing a 4 dB improvement on the downlink and a 6 dB improvement on the uplink going from Ku-band to Ka-band. Rain fade represents a more complex aspect. Nevertheless, it can be shown that in Europe, for an availability of up to 99.7%, it is still more suitable to work in Ka-band with respect to a Ku-band system.

3. Ka-band is approximately two times higher in frequency than Ku-band. The Ka and Ku bands are given as follows.

	Ka band	Ku band
Uplink	27.5 GHz to 30.0 GHz	12.75 GHz to 14.5 GHz
Downlink	17.7 GHz to 20.2 GHz	10.7 GHz to 12.75 GHz

Higher frequency also means that for a given satellite antenna aperture the beam is smaller, allowing smaller cells. Smaller cells imply a better individual coverage :

-   On the Forward Link (gateway-to-terminals) this permits to ensure that the satellite power is used efficiently on a more limited area with the required EIRP (effective isotropic radiated power) to get closer to the given user.
-   On the Return Link (terminals-to-gateway), this improves the G/T (gain-over-temperature) of the satellite ensuring that for a given bit rate smaller resources are required at the terminals in terms of RF (radio frequency) power required from the HPA (high power amplifier) and antenna aperture. All this contributes towards smaller terminals.

For a given service area, more cells can be included if the cells are smaller. On the upside, this supports a higher order of frequency reuse. Typically four colour schemes are used to ensure a good C/I (carrier to interference ratio). Four represents an acceptable compromise between the performance and the complexity of the number of antenna apertures on the satellite. Thus the spectral resources are utilised more efficiently and more system capacity can be attained for a given available spectrum.

Ka-band offers opportunities to design a payload with higher system capacity with respect to Ku-band. At the technical level, high system capacity can permit:

- increase of the data rates to and from the terminals,
- increase in quality of service,
- increase in the population of terminals within the system or
- a combination of the above

Using a traditional Ku band satellite at a premium orbital slot dedicated to DTH services would increase the subscriber fee by a factor of 5 to 10 and reduce capacity for DTH channels.

At the commercial level, these factors combine to help the Ka-band system reduce the cost of the service provision making broadband access an affordable service for the consumer market.

4 The Tooway^{TM} Service

Consumer broadband expectations are in continuous evolution for high bandwidth consuming applications such as Web TV, VoIP, music, P2P, online gaming, database and video. These applications must be accessible at higher speeds and lower prices. KA-SAT will form the cornerstone of a major new satellite infrastructure that will significantly expand capacity for consumer broadband services across Europe and the Mediterranean Basin (triple play), while providing new opportunities for local and regional television markets.

4.1 Broadband Access

Households located within KA-SAT's coverage who do not have access to ADSL will be able to benefit from Tooway™ for full satellite-based broadband connectivity. The potential ADSL un-served market for pure satellite broadband services in 2010 is estimated to be 6 million homes in Western Europe and 8 million homes in Eastern Europe.

Capitalising on the Ka-band capacity that is already available via Eutelsat's existing resource, on HOT BIRD™ 6 and the Ku-band capacity on EUROBIRD™ 3, Eutelsat has already introduced Tooway™ for consumer broadband access using the Surfbeam^{TM} system developed by ViaSat:

- HOT BIRD™ 6 was the first European commercial satellite with a Ka band payload and was a real opportunity for Eutelsat to deploy a full Ka band system in Europe as done already by WildBlue in USA, awaiting KA-SAT.
- EUROBIRD™ 3 was the first Eutelsat satellite specifically designed for broadband applications in Ku-band and offers strong coverage over Eastern parts of Europe where HOT BIRD^{TM} 6 is not able to provide Ka band Tooway^{TM} services.

The current Tooway^{TM} service definition over HOT BIRD™ 6 and EUROBIRD™ 3 is allowing download up to 2Mbps and upload up to 384Kbps. The service differentiation is done on volume consumption per month through a Fair Access Policy (FAP). To promote a fair access use of service and avoid abuse, when consumption is above volume thresholds, the service remains available but at a lower speed. More Tooway^{TM} service information is available on www.tooway.com website.

KA-SAT with the new Surfbeam^{TM} generation system from ViaSat will allow much higher throughput and volume for each subscriber at a price comparable to ADSL and cable modem connections.

4.2 The VoIP Service

Voice over IP is also an expectation of any broadband subscriber interested in good call quality at low cost, taking advantage of competition between all the VoIP operators. VoIP through Tooway^{TM} is already available and marketed by several service distributors. The new generation of Surfbeam^{TM} manufactured by ViaSat will provide the same VoIP capabilities with QoS.

4.3 TV Services

As KA-SAT will be collocated at Eutelsat's HOT BIRD™ TV premium neighborhood, the IP services delivered via Tooway™ will complement and enrich the DVB TV offer using new combined Ku/Ka-band receive terminals. Indeed as Tooway™ is delivering ADSL-like services via satellite, Tooway^{TM} subscribers will expect to be able to access IPTV services with VoD and PVR features. IPTV offers will benefit from the new techniques including DVB-S2 VCM/ACM mode and H.264 SVC coding in order to guarantee higher bit rates and quality standards.

- **DVB-S2 VCM/ACM**

  In the DVB-S2 standard, the VCM (Variable Code and Modulation) mode is defined to avoid feedback from each terminal for waveform efficiency configuration. In such a case, a specific link budget is performed for each terminal and a static efficiency is defined for each of them according to the availability needed. In this case, the adaptive linked to the evolution of the weather is lost, but there are no longer constraints for the worst link budget applied for the entire spot. The ACM (Adaptive Code and Modulation) needs a terminal feedback on the return channel and allows each terminal to receive the best efficiency related to its fading conditions.

- **H.264 SVC**

  The SVC (Scalable Video Coding) is a new feature developed for H.264 (MPEG-4 Part 10) source coding, which allows transmitting the same video sequence coded with different resolutions and/or bit rate and/or SD-HD format. SVC is being developed to be basically applied to mobile ecosystems (DVB-SH) and ADSL video services but it will have important legacy applications for IP video services over Ka band satellite systems.

  As an example, the same video sequence can be coded in SD and HD format.

  - SD 720x576i @50 Hz
  - HD 1920x1080p @ 60 Hz

Combined with SVC the HD format could be received by a terminal in clear sky conditions as the SD format could be received by another terminal affected by fading conditions (e.g. rain). In case of stringent fading conditions an SD program with lower bit rate will be available in order to maintain TV service.

Applied to satellite, the SVC feature with DVB-S2 VCM/ACM capability will allow to not multicast the full 3 programs detailed in the Fig. 4 but only one program with 3 layers protected with different efficiencies. The bit rates and the efficiencies of interest are under study.

Definition	MPEG4 encoding bit rate *under study*	DVB-S2 Efficiency *under study*	Example of quality
SD	1Mbps	QPSK 2/3 1.33	
SD	2.5Mbps	QPSK 5/6 1.66	
HD	8Mbps	8PSK 2/3 1.99	

Image source from Institut Nachrichtentechnik Heinrich-Hertz-Institut, URL : http://www. ist-ipmedianet.org/FlyerSVC.PDF.

Fig. 4. SVC feature applied on KA-SAT for new TV services

5 The Tooway™ Consumer Terminal

The consumer equipment will include an ODU (outdoor unit) with antenna diameter of less than 75 cm and a compact IDU (indoor unit) providing a simple customer interface: plug and play Ethernet and/or Wifi. The installation will employ automated tools for simplified antenna alignment and commissioning. The use of circular

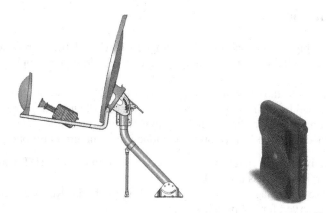

Fig. 5. The new Tooway™ Ka band customer equipment which will be used on KA-SAT satellite

polarization further simplifies the installation. The installation procedure is the same anywhere within the satellite service area and it requires no software in the PC.

As KA-SAT will be located at 13°E, joining three large HOT BIRD™ Ku-band broadcasting satellites, Eutelsat will be able to enrich the range of consumer entertainment services offered from the Group's prime neighborhood by enabling satellite homes to receive television in the Ku-band and new rich media services in the Ka-band through a single dual-band antenna which was first demonstrated at the Satexpo exhibition in Italy in 2008 (see Fig. 6).

The antenna employs a frequency selective sub reflector which is transparent to Ku band and reflecting Ka band, allowing the use of a traditional Universal LNB. Ku band reception on this modified Ka band interactive antenna is equivalent to a typical 60-70cm receive only DTH antenna.

Fig. 6. Prototype of Ka & Ku bands Tooway™ ODU

6 Conclusion

Through the high power and broad coverage of its HOT BIRD™ broadcast satellites, Eutelsat has built the world's leading video neighborhood, assembling over 1,100 channels.

In 2010 with the launch of KA-SAT, Eutelsat will triple the total capacity commercialised by its in-orbit resource and drive broadband to new frontiers.

By uniting these leading-edge Ku and Ka-band technologies at one satellite neighborhood, Eutelsat is developing a unique infrastructure in Europe able to:

- deliver a full range of digital services to consumers (DTH and interactive services such as triple play),
- take advantage of a new band (Ka) enabling Ku band capacity to be preserved for TV broadcasting,
- satisfy a real and common solution to the digital divide over the full Europe area.

Thanks to KA-SAT and the new generation Surfbeam™ system from ViaSat, the Tooway™ service will increase the throughput in services already offered to subscribers at a price comparable to ADSL and cable modem connections. Tooway™ is increasing its capabilities to satisfy customer needs.

The Ka band is really making the difference for triple play services over satellite.

Time Scheduling Based on Tradeoff between Detection Performance and QoS Requirement

Jun Sun and Hongbo Zhu

Institute of Communication Technology,
Key Laboratory of Wireless Communications,
Jiangsu Province, Nanjing University of Posts and telecommunications,
Nanjing, JiangSu, 210003
freyjajune@163.com

Abstract.[1] A time scheduling scheme satisfying both the detection performance of a cognitive node in cognitive networks and the QoS requirement of a secondary user under fading channels is proposed in this paper. First, an optimal sensing time is obtained by maximizing the achievable throughput of a secondary user under the constraint that the primary user is sufficiently protected. Then, according to the second order statistic characteristics of fading channels, the transmission time is defined under the outage capacity constraint of a secondary user. Finally, a secondary sensing time is defined for the necessary of both primary protection and the guarantee of transmission QoS. It turns out to be an efficient scheme of spectrum utilization and time scheduling.

Keywords: dynamic scheduling, cognitive node, channel characteristics, optimal sensing time, detection performance, QoS requirement.

1 Introduction

Spectrum sharing [1]-[4] is a promising and efficient technique for solving the problem of spectrum crisis. Cognitive technique, or cognitive radio [5]-[7], is considered as a necessary and key technique for the implement of spectrum sharing as well as cognitive networks. In a cognitive network, from a secondary user point of view, the maximum throughput which is necessary for a certain QoS requirement should be guaranteed when a secondary user is permitted to access a licensed spectrum band. The longer the transmission time, the more data rate a secondary user can be transmitted. However, from a primary user point of view, it is hoped that the interference from a secondary user is as little as possible. On the other words, the secondary user must sense the presence of a primary user as soon and accurate as possible. This means the detection performance correlated to the sensing time should be guaranteed for a cognitive node. The longer the sensing time, the higher detection probability can be obtained. So, the sensing

---

[1] This paper is supported by National 973 project[2007CB310600]; NNSF project[60432040]; NNSF project[60572024]; China Education Ministry Doctor Foundation[20050293003]; China Poster Doctor Foundation[20080441067]; Province Poster Doctor Foundation[0802017B], 863[2009AA011300].

K. Sithamparanathan (Ed.): Psats 2009, LNICST 15, pp. 29–36, 2009.

time for detecting the primary user and the transmission time for a secondary user is a contradiction.

There are many achievements considering some points of above problem, such as papers [8]-[13]. In [9], the authors proposed an adaptive scheduling scheme considering the channel side information (CSI) and QoS guarantee separately. In [10], the authors studied the fundamental tradeoff between sensing capability and achievable throughput and proposed the design scheme for sensing slot duration to maximize the achievable throughput under no-fading channels. Here, we consider both sides in paper [9] jointly and extend the results in [10] to fading channels. This results in a novel and more efficient time scheduling scheme which satisfies both the detection performance of a cognitive node and the QoS requirement of a secondary user under fading channels.

The paper is organized as following. Section II gives the novel scheduling scheme. The conceptions in this scheme are explained in detail in section III. The results are given in section IV. Section V is conclusions.

2   Time Scheduling Scheme

Figure 1 is the framework of our new scheduling scheme. It shows an available spectrum band for a single cognitive node of a single secondary user in one cognitive network. The time axis is divided into frames. Each frame of duration T_f is further divided into some slots. The wide gray slot duration T_s is used to sense the presence of a primary user on this spectrum band. The white slot duration T_d is used to transmit data of a secondary user. The narrow gray slot duration T_{ss} is named as secondary sensing time here which is a new definition in our scheme. At the beginning for a spectrum band, a cognitive node sensing whether the primary user is absent on this band during T_s which is optimized in the next section. If the band is free, the secondary user is permitted to transmit its data during T_d which is determined by the outage probability as well as the fading channel characteristics. This will be explained in the next section. If

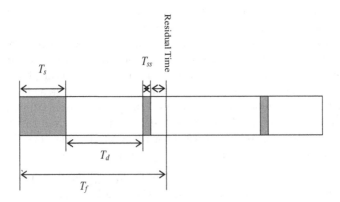

Fig. 1. The time scheduling scheme proposed in this paper

$T_s + T_d < T_f$, It is necessary in the same frame to sense the primary user again since the channel states may change because of the presence of the primary user. This sensing is done during T_{ss}. If $T_s + T_d + T_{ss} < T_f$, there is residual time in the same frame where the secondary user can continue to transmit its data sequence if the primary is absent. If $T_s + T_d \geq T_f$, T_{ss} is set in the next frame. If there is no primary user, the secondary user goes on transmitting its data in the second T_d. Then, the whole processing is in a cycle until the primary user appears again.

3 Definitions of the Parameters

3.1 Average Detection Threshold

First of all, the average detection threshold should be defined. In [14], the author gave the expressions of detection probability and false alarm probability under no-fading channels in Q functions. While, in [8], these expressions were transformed into $Erfc$ functions. Here, we use the latter format and rewrite these functions as following.

$$P_f = \frac{1}{2} Erfc(\frac{1}{\sqrt{2}} \frac{\gamma_{th1} - 2m}{\sqrt{4m}}) \tag{1}$$

$$P_d = \frac{1}{2} Erfc(\frac{1}{\sqrt{2}} \frac{\gamma_{th1} - 2m(\gamma + 1)}{\sqrt{4m(2\gamma + 1)}}) \tag{2}$$

Where, $\mathrm{Erfc}(x) = \frac{2}{\sqrt{\pi}} \int_x^\infty e^{-t^2} dt$. The quantity γ_{th1} is a chosen channel-signal-noise rate (CSNR) threshold for detection. The quantity γ is the CSNR of the primary user received at the receiver of the secondary network. The quantity m is the time-bandwidth product. If the sampling frequency of the band-pass filter is f_s which is also equal to the bandwidth of the signal and the observation interval is T_s, $m = T_s f_s$. From Equation (2), the detection threshold under no-fading channels as

$$\gamma_{th1} = 2\mathrm{Erfc}^{-1}(2\overline{P}_d)\sqrt{2m(2\gamma + 1)} + 2m(\gamma + 1) \tag{3}$$

Where, $\overline{P}_d$ is the target detection probability. In a fading channel, Equation (3) should be averaged as

$$\begin{aligned}
\overline{\gamma_{th1}} &= \int_\gamma \gamma_{th1} f_\gamma(\gamma) d\gamma \\
&= \int_\gamma [2\mathrm{Erfc}^{-1}(2\overline{P}_d)\sqrt{2m(2\gamma + 1)} + 2m(\gamma + 1)] f_\gamma(\gamma) d\gamma
\end{aligned} \tag{4}$$

Here, $f_\gamma(\gamma)$ is a probability density function (PDF) of CSNR for fading channels. For a Rayleigh channel,

$$f_\gamma(\gamma) = \frac{1}{\overline{\gamma}} e^{-\gamma/\overline{\gamma}} \tag{5}$$

Substituting (5) into (4), after some manipulation, there is

$$
\begin{aligned}
\overline{\gamma_{th1}} &= \int_{\gamma} \gamma_{th1} f_{\gamma}(\gamma) d\gamma \\
&= \frac{1}{\overline{\gamma}} \int_0^{\infty} [2\mathrm{Erfc}^{-1}(2\overline{P}_d)\sqrt{2m(2\gamma+1)} + 2m(\gamma+1)]e^{-\gamma/\overline{\gamma}} d\gamma \\
&= 4\sqrt{m\overline{\gamma}} Erfc^{-1}(2\overline{P}_d)e^{1/2\overline{\gamma}}\Gamma(\tfrac{3}{2}, \tfrac{1}{2\overline{\gamma}}) + 2m\overline{\gamma}e^{1/\overline{\gamma}}\Gamma(2, \tfrac{1}{\overline{\gamma}})
\end{aligned}
\tag{6}
$$

The quantity $\overline{\gamma}$ is the average CSNR of fading channels.

3.2   Optimal Sensing Time

According to paper [10], the achievable throughput for a secondary user is defined as

$$
R = \frac{T_f - T_s}{T_f}(1 - P_f)C_0
\tag{7}
$$

Where, C_0 denotes the throughput of the secondary user when it operates in absence of primary user. Obviously, the achievable throughput is a function of sensing time T_s. So, the optimal T_s can be obtained by the following optimization problem

$$
\begin{aligned}
\max \quad &R = \frac{T_f - T_s}{T_f}(1 - P_f)C_0 \\
s.t. \quad &P_d \geq \overline{P}_d
\end{aligned}
\tag{8}
$$

3.3   Transmission Time

To guarantee a requirement maximum throughput for a secondary user, the transmission must be under a certain outage probability which defined as [15]-[16]

$$
P_{out} = P_r\{\frac{1}{2}\log(1 + \gamma_s) < R\} \leq \varepsilon
\tag{9}
$$

Where, the parameter ε is the given outage probability and γ_s is the received CSNR at the secondary receiver. In order to guarantee the throughput R, γ_s should be greater or equal to the CSNR threshold which is defined as

$$
\gamma_{th2} = e^{2R} - 1
\tag{10}
$$

Besides, the transmission is also determined by fading channel states. Here, the data transmission time T_d for the achievable throughput of the secondary user is defined as the average fading time [17] when the CSNR of the secondary user falls in $[\gamma_{th2}, \overline{\gamma_{th1}})$, that is

$$
\overline{T}_d = \frac{p(\gamma_{th2} \leq \gamma < \overline{\gamma_{th1}})}{N_2 - N_1}
\tag{11}
$$

$$
N_j = \sqrt{\frac{2\pi\gamma_j}{\overline{\gamma}}} f_D e^{-\gamma_j/\overline{\gamma}}
\tag{12}
$$

Where, $p(\gamma_{th2} \leq \gamma < \overline{\gamma_{th1}})$ is the probability when the CSNR falls in $[\gamma_{th2}, \overline{\gamma_{th1}})$. And N_j is the level crossing rate (LCR). The expression of LCR in Rayleigh channel is defined in (12) where f_D is the maximum Doppler frequency.

3.4   Secondary Sensing Time

After T_d, the CSNR maybe changed because of the change of channel states or the presence of the primary user. It is necessary to sense the channel again. This is why to defined secondary sensing time T_{ss}. Because it is a tough sensing, it is defined as a part of T_s from the frequency efficiency point of view, that is,

$$T_{ss} = kT_s \tag{13}$$

Here, the factor k is obtained by

$$P_f = \frac{1}{2}Erfc([\sqrt{2\bar{\gamma}}Erfc^{-1}(2\overline{P}_d)e^{1/(2\bar{\gamma})}\Gamma(\frac{3}{2}, \frac{1}{2\bar{\gamma}}) + \sqrt{\frac{kT_sf_s}{2}}(\bar{\gamma}e^{1/\bar{\gamma}}\Gamma(2, \frac{1}{\bar{\gamma}}) - 1)]) \leq \overline{P}_f \tag{14}$$

Given a target false alarm probability $\overline{P}_f$, the minimum value of factor k can be obtained by solving (14). Till now, all the parameters in our time scheduling scheme in Fig.1 are determined.

4   Simulation Results

In this section, computer simulation results are presented to evaluate the time scheduling scheme satisfying both the detection performance of a cognitive node in cognitive networks and the QoS requirement of a secondary user under fading channels proposed in this paper. According to [10] and IEEE 802.22 standard, the primary user is assumed to be a M-PSK modulated signal with bandwidth of $6MHz$ and the sampling frequency is the same as the bandwidth of the primary user. The SNR for primary user received at the secondary user's receiver is $-15dB$. The frame duration $T_f = 200ms$, and the target probability of detection is assumed $P_d = 0.9$. First of all, Fig.2 shows the normalized achievable throughput for the secondary network, which is defined as $(T_f - T_s)(1 - P_f)/T_f$. It is the comparison between the result in [10] which is denoted by the real line and the result of our scheme according to (6) which is denoted by the x-mark line. It reveals a maximum point of the throughput at the sensing time of about $3.0ms$ under fading channels. It is same as that of no-fading channels case. However, the maximum value of the throughput is less than that of no-fading channels case. Then, Fig.3 shows the result of the normalized average spectral efficiency (ASE) which is defined as

$$\overline{ASE} = \frac{\sum_{i=1}^{N}\sum_{j=1}^{n}T_{d_{ij}}}{\sum_{i=1}^{N}T_{f_i}} \tag{15}$$

The parameter N denotes the number of frames and n denotes the number of data transmission duration for a secondary user. The real line denotes the result using the new scheme proposed in Fig.1 of this paper. The x-mark line denotes the result of optimal CSI-based scheduling policy shown in [9]. It reveals that the new scheme can obtain a higher ASE than that of CSI-based scheme especially at low average CSNR.

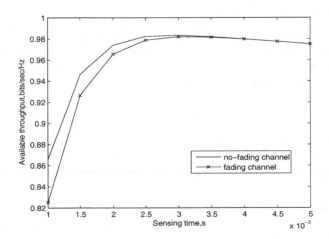

Fig. 2. The normalized achievable throughput for a secondary user

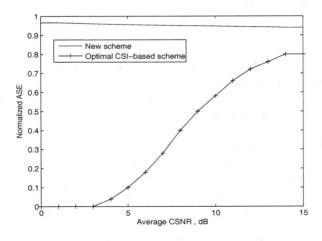

Fig. 3. The normalized ASE for a secondary user

5   Conclusions

In this paper, we propose a time scheduling scheme satisfying both the detection performance in cognitive networks and the QoS requirement of a secondary user under fading channels. The optimal sensing time is obtained under the new defined detection threshold in fading channels. Both the simulation result and the theoretic result show that the maximum throughput of the secondary user corresponding optimal sensing time exists. The optimal sensing time duration is the same for both no-fading channels and fading channels. But the maximum throughput is different for two cases. The normalized ASE shows that the new scheduling scheme can obtain a higher ASE than that of the current optimal scheme. It is necessary to research the frame error rate and power efficiency for both the secondary network and the primary network in our scheme for our future work.

References

1. Yamada, T., Cosovic, I., Maeda, K., Kaiser, S.: Misallocation-Averse Policy for Decentralized Resource Allocation in Spectrum Sharing Systems. In: 3rd International Conference on Cognitive Radio Oriented Wireless Networks and Communications, pp. 1–6 (2008)
2. Ji, Z., Liu, K.J.R.: Cognitive Radios for Dynamic Spectrum Access - Dynamic Spectrum Sharing: A Game Theoretical Overview. IEEE Communications Magazine 45(5), 88–94 (2007)
3. Xu, Y., Chen, W., Cao, Z.: Optimal Power Allocation for Spectrum Sharing in Frequency-Selective Unlicensed Bands. IEEE Communications Letters 12(7), 511–513 (2008)
4. Etkin, R., Parekh, A., Tse, D.: Spectrum Sharing for Unlicensed Bands. IEEE Journal on Selected Areas in Communications 25(3), 517–528 (2007)
5. Mitola, J., Maguire, G.Q.: Cognitive Radio: Makeing Software Radios More Personal. IEEE Pers. Commun. 6(6), 13–18 (1999)
6. Shankar, N.S., Cordeiro, C., Challapali, K.: Spectrum Agile Radios: Utilization and Sensing Architectures. In: Proc. IEEE Symp. New Frontiers in Dynamic Spectrum Access Networks, Baltimore, USA, pp. 160–169 (2005)
7. Tian, Z., Giannakis, G.B.: A Wavelet Approach to Wideband Spectrum Sensing for Cognitive Radios. In: Proc. Int. Conf. on Cognitive Radio Oriented Wireless Networks and Communications, Greece, pp. 8–10 (2006)
8. Ghasemi, A., Sousa, E.S.: Spectrum Sensing in Cognitive Radio Networks: the Cooperation-processing Tradeoff. Wirel. Commnun. Mob. Comput. 7, 1049–1060 (2007), doi:10.1002/wcm
9. Hoang, A.T., Liang, Y.-C.: Adaptive Scheduling of Spectrum Sensing Periods in Cognitive Radio Networks. In: IEEE Global Telecommunications Conference, GLOBECOM 2007, pp. 3128–3132 (2007)
10. Liang, Y.-C., Zeng, Y., Peh, E., Hoang, A.T.: Sensing-throughput Tradeoff for Cognitive Radio Networks. In: IEEE International Conference on Communications ICC 2007, pp. 5330–5334 (2007)
11. Ghasemi, A., Sousa, E.S.: Asymptotic Performance of Collaborative Spectrum Sensing under Correlated Log-normal Shadowing. IEEE Communications Letters 11(1), 34–36 (2007)
12. Ghasemi, A., Sousa, E.S.: Fundamental Limits of Spectrum-sharing in Fading Environments. IEEE Transactions on Wireless Communications 6(2), 649–658 (2007)
13. Kang, X., Liang, Y.-C., Garg, H.K.: Outage Probability Minimization under Both The Transmit and Interference Power Constraints for Fading Channels in Cognitive Radio Networks. In: IEEE International Conference on Communications Workshops, ICC Workshops 2008, pp. 482–486 (2008)
14. Digham, F.F., Alouini, M.S., Simon, M.K.: On the Energy Detection of Unkown Signals over Fading Channels. In: Proceedings of the IEEE International Conference on Communications (ICC), pp. 3575–3579 (2003)

15. Kang, X., Liang, Y.-C., Garg, H.K.: Outage Probability Minimization under Both The Transmit and Interference Power Constraints for Fading Channels in Cognitive Radio Networks. In: IEEE International Conference on Communications Workshops, ICC Workshops 2008, pp. 482–486 (2008)
16. Kang, X., Liang, Y.-C., Nallanathan, A.: Optimal Power Allocation for Fading Channels in Cognitive Radio Networks: Delay-Limited Capacity and Outage Capacity. In: IEEE Vehicular Technology Conference, VTC Spring 2008, pp. 1544–1548 (2008)
17. Goldsmith, A.: Wireless Communications. Cambridge University Press, Cambridge (2005)

Study of the Quantum Channel between Earth and Space for Satellite Quantum Communications

Cristian Bonato, Andrea Tomaello, Vania Da Deppo, Giapiero Naletto,
and Paolo Villoresi

Department of Information Engineering, University of Padova (Italy)
CNR-INFM LUXOR Laboratory for Ultraviolet and X-ray, Padova (Italy)
{bonatocr,andrea.tomaello,paolo.villoresi}@dei.unipd.it

Abstract. In this work there are studied the conditions for the effective quantum communications between a terminal on Earth and the other onboard of an orbiter. The quantum key distribution between a LEO satellite and a ground station is studied in particular. The effect of the propagation over long distances as well as the background during day or night is modeled, compared and discussed in the context of key generation and exchange.

Keywords: Quantum cryptography – Satellite optical communications – single photon transmission.

1 Introduction

The quantum limit is the natural frontier for space communication. With a quantum channel the information is encoded in the state of a single entity, in the following a photon. On Earth, this was extended to links with length of about one hundred kilometres. In the case of fibre links, this is due to the signal attenuation in the fibre; in the case of free-space link the losses are due to atmospheric turbulence and absorption. Free-space optical terminals exploiting satellite-based relays are the only resource that can enable global scale quantum key distribution, since single photon propagation is for the main part in vacuum with no turbulence or absorption, and just a small part of the path is through the atmosphere. Several proof-of-principle experiments have been carried out recently: among these the feasibility of single-photon exchange between a satellite and an optical ground station was demonstrated in 2008 [1].

2 Signal and Noise in the Quantum Channel

Several aspects of the space quantum channel deserve careful attention in order to provide a complete picture of a quantum space link.

Signal Attenuation. The main factor limiting the performance of free-space optical communication is atmospheric turbulence, both for terrestrial horizontal links or for links between ground and satellites. Turbulent eddies whose size is large compared to the size of the beam induce a deflection of the beam (beam wandering), while

K. Sithamparanathan (Ed.): Psats 2009, LNICST 15, pp. 37–40, 2009.

smaller-scale turbulent features induce beam broadening. In other words, observing a beam which propagates through turbulent atmosphere at different time instants, one can see a broadened beam randomly deflected in different directions. When integrating the observation over a time-scale longer than the beam-wandering characteristic time, the global effect is a broadening of the beam. For a Gaussian beam of waist w_0 and intensity I_0, the long-term intensity distribution is described by [2]:

$$< I(r, L) >= I_0 e^{-2r^2/w_{LT}^2}$$

where:

$$w_{LT}^2 = w_{ST}^2 + 2 < \beta^2 >$$

w_{LT} is the long-term beam width, w_{ST} is the short-term one and β is the instantaneous beam displacement from the unperturbed position.

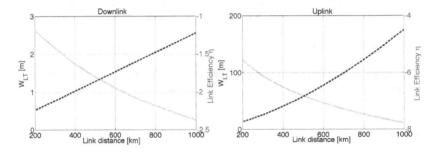

Fig. 1. Beam width w_{LT} and link efficiency for the uplink and the downlink

The results are shown in Fig. 1 for the uplink and the downlink. For the uplink, the beam first propagates through the turbulent atmosphere and then, aberrated, in vacuum, resulting in a large broadening (around 100 m diameter at 500 km). For the downlink, the beam propagates through turbulence only in the final stage, and the spreading is much less (around 1 m at 500 km). Therefore, the attenuation is much stronger in the uplink (more than 50 dB for a 30-cm diameter telescope) compared to the downlink (around 10 dB).

Background noise. As regards the expected background noise in the uplink, during day-time the main contribution is given by sunlight reflection on the Earth surface into the telescope field-of-view. We calculated this contribution to be between 10^7-10^9 photons per second (for a 1 nm of bandwidth). During night-time the main sources of noise are moonlight reflection from the Earth surface, which we calculated as six-orders of magnitude less than it is in day-time (around 10^1-10^3 photons per second) and light pollution from human activities.

We show that the signal-to-noise ratio is proportional to:

$$SNR = \frac{\epsilon_S}{\epsilon_N} \propto \frac{\eta_0}{w_{LT}^2 (IFOV)^2 \Delta\nu\Delta t}$$

where η_0 comprises the detection efficiency, the pointing losses and the atmospheric attenuation, (IFOV) is the telescope field of view and Δt is the detector gating time. In first approximation the SNR does not depend on the radius R of the receiving telescope. The results show that during day-time it is impossible to achieve a SNR higher than 1. During night-time a good SNR can be obtained both for the uplink (~15 dB) and the downlink (~20 dB), provided that a strong filtering is implemented.

3 Key Generation Rate

The expected key generation rates results a function of the link distance for different configurations (uplink, downlink) during night-time for different quantum key distribution protocol.

In most practical quantum communication experiments, single photons are implemented with weak coherent pulses, which have a non-zero probability of multi-photon emission. On such multi-photon pulses Eve could perform a photon-number-splitting attack (PNS)[3]. In the case of high-loss channels, like the ground-to-satellite one, multi-photon pulses are more likely to survive the channel attenuation and get to Bob's detector than single-photon pulses. The probability of tagged bits in the key, for which Eve can have information without introducing any perturbation, is very high. In the case of the BB84 protocol, a worst-case estimate is taken on the fraction of tagged bits, assuming that all multi-photon pulses are correctly intercepted by Eve. In this case the only way to guarantee security is to reduce the probability of having multi-photon pulses, reducing the source mean photon number. This results in the impossibility to establish a BB84 uplink to a LEO satellite, while for the downlink the results are much better (see Fig. 2).

A better estimate of the fraction of tagged bits can be obtained using weak pulses with different mean photon numbers, the decoy-state technique [4]. Such technique mitigates the need to have a very low intensity source, so that a meaningful key generation rate can be achieved even in the uplink (Fig. 2). Assuming a three-intensities decoy state protocol (vacuum, $\mu = 0.27$, $\mu' = 0.4$) a key generation rate of 10^{-6} can be obtained for an uplink to a satellite orbiting at 350 km (see Fig. 2). The cut-off distance for un uplink is around 300-400 km (depending on the QBER).

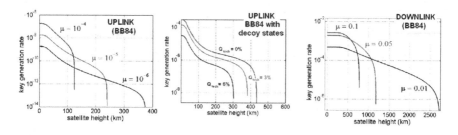

Fig. 2. Key generation rate for uplink (BB84 with and without decoy states) and downlink (BB84). For the uplink, it is possible to establish a QKD channel only using the decoy-state technique and the cut-off distance is around 300-400 km.

The establishment of an entanglement-based link between a LEO satellite and Earth is also investigated. In this case the most important parameter is the SNR [4]: only achieving a 6:1 SNR Bell inequalities can be violated.. We show that a configuration with one local receiver and the other to or from a LEO satellite is feasible. The configuration with two downlinks [5] is also be feasible, but with very strict hardware requirements.

In conclusion, satellite technology is expected to provide the means for the extension of quantum communication on the global scale.

Acknowledgments. The authors would like to thank Prof. Cesare Barbieri, Prof. Gianfranco Cariolaro, Dr. Ivan Capraro, Dr. Tommaso Occhipinti, Dr. Fabrizio Tamburini, Dr. Gabriele Anzolin of University of Padova for helpful discussions. This work has been carried out within the Strategic-Research-Project QUINTET of the Department of Information Engineering, University of Padova.

References

[1] Villoresi, P., et al.: Experimental verification of the feasibility of a quantum channel between space and Earth. New Journal of Physics 10, 033038 (2008)
[2] Dios, F., et al.: Scintillation and beam-wander analysis in an optical ground station-satellite uplink. Appl. Opt. 43, 3866–3873 (2004)
[3] Lo, H.-K., Ma, X., Chen, K.: Decoy state quantum key distribution. Phys. Rev. Lett. 94, 230504 (2005)
[4] Aspelmeyer, M., et al.: Long distance quantum communication with entangled photons using satellites. IEEE Sel. Top. In Quantum Electronics 9, 1541 (2003)
[5] Armengol, J., et al.: Quantum communications at ESA: towards a space experiment on the ISS. Acta Astronautica 63, 165 (2008)

Spectral Analysis of Experimental Ka-Band Propagation Measurements over the Australian LEO Microsatellite 'FedSat'

Thorsten Kostulski and Sam Reisenfeld

University of Technology, Sydney, Centre for Real-time Information Networks (CRIN)
P.O. Box 123, Broadway NSW 2007, Australia
{Thorsten.Kostulski,samr}@uts.edu.au

Abstract. The increased interest in the use of Ka band frequencies in satellite communications has prompted extensive propagation studies and the development of several rain fade models in the past, all of which are based on measurements from geostationary satellites only. Based on novel data, which has been experimentally obtained from the low earth orbit microsatellite 'FedSat', this paper addresses the spectral analysis of variable slant-path attenuation measurements under various weather conditions by examples, compares the results to similar GEO statistics and identifies potentially significant effects.

Keywords: Ka band, low earth orbit, satellite propagation, attenuation, spectral analysis, scintillation, rain fading.

1 Introduction

Motivated by bandwidth shortage in the classical satellite communication frequency bands (C, X, Ku), several experiments were undertaken to investigate the propagation conditions in the K/Ka band (18-36 GHz), predominantly in the years between 1974 and 1993 [1]. Signals at Ka band frequencies are severely affected by hydrometeors, e.g. rain and ice, and extensive empirical studies were conducted in order to model the statistics of signal attenuation and fade slopes. The data obtained from experimental, *geostationary* (GEO) satellites like ACTS, OLYMPUS and ITALSAT, in conjunction with the worldwide collection of precipitation data, has significantly contributed to the formation of widely used propagation models, such as the Crane model and various ITU Recommendations [2].

In recent years, low earth orbit (LEO) satellites and satellite constellations carrying Ka band payloads have increasingly emerged due to notable advantages in signal latency, launch cost, system capacity and earth station mobility. Since previously established propagation models were based on geostationary satellite measurements only, the demand has risen to adapt those models to LEO satellites. However, as a result of the dissimilar orbital characteristics, any measurements require the implementation of both spatial and frequency tracking in an earth station design. In contrast to the observation of significant rain events using ubiquitous GEO satellites,

K. Sithamparanathan (Ed.): Psats 2009, LNICST 15, pp. 41–48, 2009.

the extremely reduced visibility of any one LEO satellite would have to coincide with any such event, making the successful data collection a very challenging undertaking.

The propagation measurement records of previous Ka band LEO satellite missions have been kept classified, commercial-in-confidence (Iridium, Teledesic) or sparsely published for unknown reasons (ROCSAT). The 2002 launch of the Australian LEO microsatellite 'FedSat' with a Ka band transponder payload represents the first and only mission with the goal of collecting and publishing Ka band propagation data from a LEO microsatellite [3]. Subsequent to the presentation and interpretation of attenuation phenomena in [4] and [5], this paper examines the fade slope and power spectral density statistics of received beacon and bent pipe mode signals under various weather conditions. It will be demonstrated that the knowledge of fade statistics is essential for the selection of the most suitable modulation scheme and therefore for optimum Ka band LEO satellite link design and performance.

2 Experimental Platform

2.1 Spacecraft and Earth Station

The research platform consists of the spacecraft and a fast-tracking earth station located in Sydney, Australia. Selected specifications of the satellite and its orbital properties are summarised in Table 1, most importantly the short orbital period and the very low transmit power. FedSat was designed and constructed almost entirely in Australia and carries various other experimental payloads besides the Ka band transponder.

Table 1. Selected orbital properties and Ka band payload specifications of FedSat

FedSat specifications		Ka band payload specifications	
Catalog No.	28598, 'FedSat'	Uplink frequency	29.93 GHz
Structure	50 cm cube, 58 kg	Downlink frequency	21.13 GHz
Inclination	98.5°	Transmit power	–6 dBW
Mean altitude	800 km	Antenna type	Multi-mode horns
Orbital period	100.85 min	U/L antenna gain	7.25 dB (max.)
Stabilisation	3-axis	D/L antenna gain	6.15 dB (max.)
Average power	35 W (per orbit)	Antenna beamwidth	120° isoflux approx.
Launch	14 Dec 2002 (Japan)	Receiver front end	Custom MMIC
Design lifetime	3 years	Operation modes	Beacon mode
Actual lifetime	4 years 10 months		Bent pipe mode

The corresponding earth station was designed for both Ka band data communication and propagation experiments. Budget restraints dictated the in-house design of the majority of the functional components, in particular the high-precision, electro-mechanical tracking system, the DSP-based, blind Doppler tracking subsystem and the entire real-time control and analysis software. Resulting from FedSat's near-polar LEO orbit, an X-over-Y tracking pedestal has been designed instead of a classical Az/El mount in order to overcome the keyhole problem. A functional block diagram of the earth station and a photo of the tracking pedestal are shown in Fig. 1.

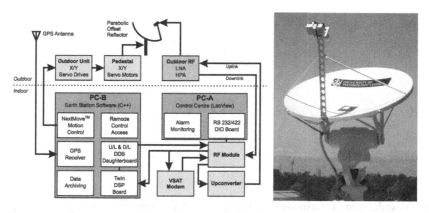

Fig. 1. Functional block diagram of the earth station (left), deployed outdoor unit (right)

In order to track the weak 20.13 GHz downlink signal transmitted by the rapidly moving spacecraft, the earth station design had to focus on accurate timing, high-precision spatial tracking, rapid signal acquisition and low-SNR frequency tracking. Due to the low downlink power budget, a dynamic tracking accuracy of 0.1° had to be maintained at all times, while using pointing angles pre-calculated from orbital elements. A novel, high-performance frequency estimation algorithm has been developed for the acquisition of the unknown carrier in noise and for subsequent Doppler shift compensation in the RF circuit [6]. The power level of the received signal was initially recorded at 70 ms intervals (f_s=14 Hz), which was later enhanced to 6.7 ms intervals (f_s=150 Hz) in order to capture rapid scintillations. For comparison, 'high sampling rate' measurements on ACTS were made at 20 Hz [7].

2.2 Pass Operation and Data Collection

Unlike preceding propagation experiments over GEO satellites, LEO satellite passes only allow the observation of a relatively short duration of around 15 minutes maximum. In the FedSat case, when elevation masking (30° design limit) and low-elevation passes are taken into account, this interval is reduced to an average data record of only 5-10 minutes. Due to the earth rotation, the trajectory changes for each pass, and only very few theoretically visible passes higher than the required minimum elevation are actually long enough for data collection, as illustrated in Fig. 2. When operational restraints, such as the spacecraft power budget and resource sharing, are taken into account, the number of *practically* usable passes reduces to an average of 2 per week, or 7% of all visible passes. Compared to GEO experiments, this represents only 0.2% of the potential recording time. The presented statistics demonstrate that the chance of a pass occurring during significant events, like a rain storm, is exceedingly small, making the collection of meaningful data far more difficult for the LEO case. On the positive side, a trajectory from horizon to horizon means that it is possible to observe a variety of different weather conditions (rain, clouds, clear sky) during the same pass. For each experiment, the prevailing weather conditions along the trajectory and possible precipitation were recorded.

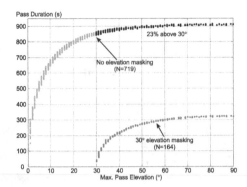

Fig. 2. Pass duration vs. maximum elevation statistics for all visible passes (top) and for passes with a 30° elevation mask (bottom) over a 200-day period

During the 30 months of earth station operation, 84 experiments have been conducted for various purposes. Usable propagation data was collected on 28 occasions and during various weather conditions. The majority of the recorded passes represent beacon mode reception, i.e. propagation effects on the 20.13 GHZ downlink only. While this number of passes is too small for the proposal of an independent, empirical propagation model, several interesting attenuation, scintillation and low-angle fading phenomena have been observed (see Section 3).

The sampled propagation data is time-stamped, power-calibrated and processed on a 32-bit floating-point DSP. Subsequently, free-space path loss is subtracted, and additional attenuation introduced by the squint angle, i.e. the earth station receiver moving out of the satellite's footprint, is taken into account by modelling the spacecraft antenna gain pattern. In some cases, the signal was tracked less than 6° elevation on the descending path, which is below the design limit and therefore well outside the intended isoflux antenna footprint. In all cases, the accuracy of nadir pointing was confirmed through telemetry from FedSat's attitude control system.

3 Propagation Measurement Results

The collected data has been analysed in terms of atmospheric attenuation effects and power spectral density (PSD). In order to facilitate the understanding of LEO pass measurements, a time-domain example will be discussed first. Further charts can be found in [4] and [5].

3.1 Time-Domain Analysis

Fig. 3 gives an example of a LEO pass recorded over 8 min 50 sec during inhomogeneous weather conditions, with a 6/8 stratus cloud cover on the ascending path, several isolated rain cells (approx. 5 mm/h) in the immediate vicinity and a light rain band on the descending path. The range varies between 872 km at maximum elevation (67°) and 2745 km at loss-of-signal (LOS). The small rain cells introduce a distinctive, localised rise in atmospheric attenuation of 5-6 dB, but do not appear to

Lecture Notes in Computer Science 5700

Commenced Publication in 1973
Founding and Former Series Editors:
Gerhard Goos, Juris Hartmanis, and Jan van Leeuwen

Editorial Board

Jens Palsberg (Ed.)

Semantics and Algebraic Specification

Essays Dedicated to Peter D. Mosses
on the Occasion of His 60th Birthday

 Springer

Volume Editor

Jens Palsberg
University of California, Los Angeles
Department of Computer Science
4531K Boelter Hall, Los Angeles, CA 90095-1596, USA
E-mail: palsberg@ucla.edu

The cover illustration showing a view of Udine was retrieved from
http://commons.wikimedia.org/wiki/File:Old_udine.jpg

Library of Congress Control Number: 2009933274

CR Subject Classification (1998): F.3.2, F.3-4, D.2, D.1.5-6, I.2, I.1.3

LNCS Sublibrary: SL 1 – Theoretical Computer Science and General Issues

ISSN   0302-9743

ISBN 978-3-642-04163-1 Springer Berlin Heidelberg New York

springer.com

© Springer-Verlag Berlin Heidelberg 2009

Typesetting: Camera-ready by author, data conversion by Scientific Publishing Services, Chennai, India
Printed on acid-free paper   SPIN: 12750504   06/3180   5 4 3 2 1 0

Peter D. Mosses

Preface

Peter Mosses, renowned researcher of Semantics of Programming Languages and Algebraic Specification Frameworks, turned 60 years old on November 3, 2008. To honor this event, many of Peter's coauthors, collaborators, close colleagues, and former students gathered in Udine, Italy on September 10, 2009 for a symposium in his honor. The presentations were on subjects related to Peter's many technical contributions and they were a tribute to his lasting impact on the field. Here is the program of the symposium:

- Opening: Jens Palsberg
- Session 1: (Chair: José Luiz Fiadeiro)
  - David Watt, Action Semantics in Retrospect
  - Hélène Kirchner, Component-Based Security Policy Design with Colored Petri Nets
  - José Meseguer, Order-Sorted Parameterization and Induction
- Session 2: (Chair: Andrzej Tarlecki)
  - Martin Musicante, An implementation of Object-Oriented Action Semantics in Maude
  - Christiano Braga, A Constructive Semantics for Basic Aspect Constructs
  - Bartek Klin, Structural Operational Semantics for Weighted Transition Systems
- Session 3:
  - Fernando Orejas, On the Specification and Verification of Model Transformations
  - Olivier Danvy, Towards Compatible and Interderivable Semantic Specifications for the Scheme Programming Language
  - Mark van den Brand, Type Checking Evolving Languages with MSOS
  - Edward Hermann Haeusler, Action Algebras and Model Algebras in Denotational Semantics
- Closing: Peter Mosses

Many thanks to Marina Lenisa from the University of Udine who coordinated the local arrangements. We also thank the Amga spa and the Net spa of Udine, the Municipality of Udine, the International Centre for Mechanical Sciences of Udine, and the Fondazione Crup for their financial support.

The 17 invited chapters of this Festschrift represent the proceedings of the symposium. Some contributors were unable to attend the event. The papers were reviewed by Philippe Bonnet, Doina Bucur, Will Clinger, Olivier Danvy, Edward Hermann Haeusler, Bartek Klin, Paddy Krishnan, Lars Kristensen, Søren Lassen, José Meseguer, Lasse R. Nielsen, Scott Owens, Jens Palsberg, Davide Sangiorgi, David Schmidt, Trian Serbanuta, Andrzej Tarlecki, and Claus Thrane. The reviewers provided feedback to the authors that helped them improve the papers.

Jill Edwards, Sara Fenn, Andy Gimblett, Will Harwood, Markus Roggenbach, and Monika Seisenberger provided a wealth of great photos of Peter. Special thanks to Olivier Danvy and José Luiz Fiadeiro for encouragement and help, and to Christopher Mosses, Peter's son, for helping to pick the photo of Peter that appears in this Festschrift.

September 2009   Jens Palsberg

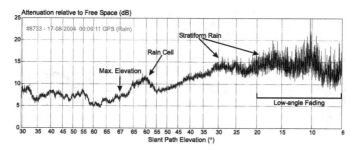

Fig. 3. Beacon signal attenuation recorded in the presence of scattered rain cells and stratiform rain, plotted in the time-domain versus the slant-path elevation angle, f_s=14 Hz. The effects of localized rain attenuation and severe low-angle fading are clearly evident.

cause a significant increase in high-frequency fading. On the descending path, below 30°, the long slant path through the stratiform rain produces a significant rise in attenuation, and also an increase in scintillation of approximately 5 dB magnitude (low angle fading). Below 10° elevation, another interesting effect can be observed: Despite a longer path through the atmosphere, the measured average attenuation actually *decreases*, while very deep fades in excess of 10 dB occur. This is an indication of terrestrial multipathing, which limits the spectral efficiency of satellite links at very low elevation angles, and particularly on low link budgets.

3.2 Power Spectra Analysis

This section compares power spectral densities for data recorded during various weather conditions. While long-term statistics are readily available for GEO satellite experiments, the results presented in this section have been obtained from single LEO satellite passes with typically less than 10 minutes of data. In order to separate low-angle fading from other propagation effects, the data from each pass has been divided into two sets, *above* and *below* the 30° design limit. In the following figures, the dark trace represents samples recorded during high elevation, whereas the light trace corresponds to samples from below 30°. No windowing or interpolation has been applied, since this can lead to distortion. Three beacon mode examples at different weather conditions and one data set obtained from a bent pipe mode pass are shown.

Beacon Mode Measurements. In beacon mode, the Ka band transponder transmits a continuous carrier signal on 20.13 GHz. Meteorological data, including publicly available precipitation information and rain radar images, are recorded along with the pass information.

Clear Sky Conditions. The PSD in Fig. 4 was calculated from a pass on a clear, low-humidity day over 9 min 30 sec. An approximate frequency asymptote is also indicated. The graph shows the familiar decay of the spectral components with a first-order characteristic. The fairly similar high-frequency power levels of both high-angle and low-angle samples lead to the conclusion that not much turbulence was present in the atmosphere during the pass. There is no evidence of low-angle fading effects.

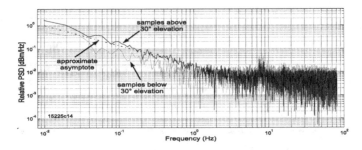

Fig. 4. PSD of a typical clear sky pass (max. elevation 83°, LOS at 14°, f_s=150 Hz)

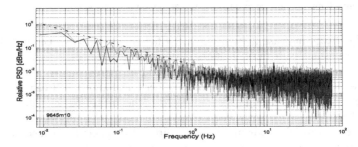

Fig. 5. PSD of a pass with 8/8 stratus cloud cover (max. elevation 61°, LOS at 10°, f_s=150 Hz)

Cloudy Conditions. Fig. 5 shows the PSD representation of a LEO pass during overcast conditions with a thick stratus cloud cover, but no precipitation. The characteristics, such as 1st order behaviour and low/high angle power levels, are similar to the clear sky case, however scintillations are slightly higher around 1 Hz.

Rain Cells. The example in Fig. 6 represents the PSD of the same pass as in Section 3.1 (Fig. 3). Despite the lower sampling rate, the comparison between the high and the low-angle PSD leads to interesting observations. Both PSDs exhibit the same asymptotic slope as in the other cases, however there is no distinct corner frequency for the high-elevation section. The low-angle PSD segment appears to level out one order of magnitude earlier than without precipitation, which is a clear indication of rain fade occurring along a very long effective path. In addition, the

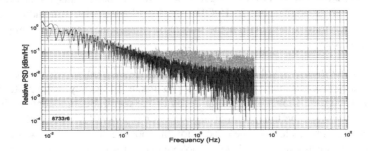

Fig. 6. PSD of the rain-affected beacon pass from Fig. 3 (max. el. 67°, LOS at 6°, f_s=14 Hz)

power level of high-frequency components is considerably elevated, which means that high-frequency scintillations introduced by rain at low elevation angles are very significant. This observation has far-reaching implications on the optimum utilisation of the channel capacity, as discussed in [8].

Bent Pipe Mode Measurements. The traces in Fig. 7 have been derived from a bent pipe mode pass during overcast conditions. In this operation mode, a Doppler pre-corrected uplink carrier signal is transmitted by the earth station and therefore received by the LEO satellite at a fixed frequency of 29.93 GHz. On the uplink, the signal is already affected by tropospheric attenuation and fading. After frequency conversion and amplification by the Ka band transponder, it is re-transmitted on the 20.13 GHz downlink, where it is subjected to more channel attenuation and fading.

The plot illustrates the *composite* effect of uplink and downlink attenuation. Both PDSs tend to follow the same asymptotic slope and power level (at higher frequencies) as in the beacon mode example, however the 'corner' is less pronounced.

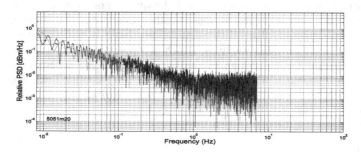

Fig. 7. PSD of a bent pipe mode experiment (max. el. 62°, LOS at 20°, f_S=14 Hz)

4 Validation of Results

4.1 Comparison with PSD Results from GEO Satellite Experiments

Since the results introduced in this paper are amongst the first in the field of LEO Ka band propagation, validation *in principle* is sought from the very well published area of Ka band propagation over GEO satellites. Due to the nature of LEO passes, the observation time was restricted to several minutes only, limiting the analysis of low-frequency components to those above 0.01 Hz.

When comparing LEO with GEO data and models [9], it is important to recall that all samples were recorded during *rapid* movement of the satellite across the sky, which implies a superposition of signal fluctuations due to spacecraft motion and of tropospheric effects, such as absorption and scattering by hydrometeors in a turbulent channel. Figs. 17 and 18 in [7] show two PSD charts obtained from a Ka band beacon on a GEO satellite (ACTS) at two separate locations, sampled at 20 Hz. At Norman, Oklahoma (OK), the fixed elevation angle was 49.1°, and at Fairbanks, Alaska (AK), the fixed elevation angle was 7.9°. The observation period of each event is comparable to the duration of a typical LEO pass. The authors state that the PSDs are consistent with theoretical predictions of clear sky, cloudy and light rain conditions.

For atmospheric conditions without heavy precipitation, both LEO and GEO results follow a similar curve shape (asymptote, 1st order characteristic). At higher elevation angles (OK), the 'corner frequency' lies at about 0.6 Hz, whereas for a longer path through the atmosphere (AK), it moves above 1 Hz with a less pronounced 'corner'. The latter observation is consistent with the results presented in this paper. The slightly rounder decay exhibited in *bent pipe mode* can be explained by Fig. 17 in [7], in which the 27 GHz PSD rolls off slightly slower than the 20 GHz PSD. These comparisons with GEO data suggest a general validity of the results, however some effects, especially the significantly raised, high-frequency power levels at low elevation angles during rain require further investigation in a LEO context.

5   Conclusion

The successful collection of scarce Ka band data from the LEO microsatellite 'FedSat' provides a new opportunity for the investigation of propagation effects. This paper has presented several power spectral density graphs of received beacon and bent pipe mode signals under various weather conditions. In some cases, the measured data suggests that LEO scintillations have a wider bandwidth than previously observed on GEO satellites, which is a potentially important finding and may be significant for the design of multi-level modulation schemes and for the selection of sustainable data rates on future Ka band LEO satellite links. Forthcoming work will include the investigation of fade slope distributions and the statistical modelling of the observed effects.

References

1. Chakraborty, D., Davarian, F., Stutzman, W.L.: The Ka-Band Propagation Measurement Campaign at JPL. IEEE Ant. and Prop. Magazine 35(1), 7–12 (1993)
2. Crane, R.K., Dissanayake, A.W.: ACTS Propagation Experiment: Attenuation Distribution Observations and Prediction Model Comparison. IEEE Proc. 85(6), 879–892 (1997)
3. Kostulski, T., Reisenfeld, S.: Ka band Propagation Experiments on the Australian Low-Earth Orbit Microsatellite 'FedSat'. In: 6th Australian Communication Theory Workshop, Brisbane, Qld, pp. 95–99 (2005)
4. Kostulski, T., Reisenfeld, S.: Variable Slant-Path Ka-Band Propagation Measurements on the Australian LEO Microsatellite 'FedSat'. In: 11th Ka and Broadband Communications Conference, Rome, pp. 365–372 (2005)
5. Kostulski, T.: Ka Band Propagation Experiments on the Australian Low Earth Orbit Microsatellite 'FedSat', PhD Thesis (Engineering), Univ. of Technology, Sydney (2008)
6. Reisenfeld, S.: A Highly Accurate Algorithm for the Estimation of the Frequency of a Complex Exponential in Additive Gaussian Noise. In: 5th Australian Communications Theory Workshop, Newcastle, NSW, pp. 154–158 (2004)
7. Mayer, C.E., Jaeger, B.E., Crane, R.K., Wang, X.: Ka-Band Scintillations: Measurements and Model Predictions. IEEE Proc. 85(6), 936–945 (1997)
8. Miodrag, F., Vilar, E.: Optimum Utilization of the Channel Capacity of a Satellite Link in the Presence of Amplitude Scintillations and Rain Attenuation. IEEE Trans. Comm. 38(11), 1958–1965 (1990)
9. Gremont, B.C., Miodrag, F.: Spatio-Temporal Rain Attenuation Model for Application to Fade Mitigation Techniques. IEEE Trans. Ant. Prop. 52(5), 1245–1256 (2004)

Satellite Broadband Revolution: How Latest Ka-Band Systems Will Change the Rules of the Industry. An Interpretation of the Technological Trajectory

Fabio Valle

Eutelsat,
70 Rue Balard, 75015 Paris, France
fvalle@eutelsat.fr

Abstract. The paper analyzes the satellite broadband systems for consumer from the perspective of technological innovation. The suggested interpretation relies upon such concepts as technological paradigm, technological trajectory and salient points. Satellite technology for broadband is a complex system on which each component (i.e. the satellite, the end-user equipment, the on-ground systems and related infrastructure) develops at different speed. Innovation in this industry concentrates recently on satellite space aircraft that seemed to be the component with the highest perceived opportunity for improvement. The industry has designed recently satellite systems with continuous dimensional increase of capacity available, suggesting that there is a technological trajectory in this area, similar to Moore's law in the computer industry. The implications for industry players, Ka-band systems, and growth of future applications are also examined.

Keywords: Technological Innovation, Value Added Services, Broadband satellite technology, Technical change, Ka-band and emerging frequency bands, Technological trajectory.

1 Introduction

After the announcement in January 2008 of the investment from ViaSat and Eutelsat in 2 high-capacity Ka-band satellites to bring satellite broadband connectivity for a joint investment of more than 700 Million US Dollars, major industry experts and analysts have noted that this investment have the potential to transform the satellite industry [1, 2]. As we will see in the following pages the technological improvement of the latest systems indicates that it represents a revolution for the satellite broadband industry.

The paper analyzes the technical trajectory of satellite broadband systems for consumer from the perspective of technological innovation. The aim is to interpret why and how the technological innovation coming from the new Ka-band system is going to modify the industry.

K. Sithamparanathan (Ed.): Psats 2009, LNICST 15, pp. 49–60, 2009.

2 Inside the Innovation Black-Box

As economists became more and more aware that innovation is crucial to economic growth and increase in productivity, they increasingly have focused on the key drivers of innovation, to open the "innovation black-box" [3]. Some very useful conceptual tools have been developed to understand the paradigm behind the innovation, partners and trajectories or [4], the epistemology of engineering [5] and how these concepts can be applied to the economic systems (e.g. [6]) and companies.

This economic/technological literature helps engineers, policy makers, managers and technologists to anticipate where innovation can happen, thus to govern and promote technical progress to the extent to which this is possible.

2.1 Technological Paradigm and Technological Trajectory

In the technological/research community the focus of technologists and engineers is normally concentrated on the recognized critical problems, following the well know concept of paradigm for technological revolutions [5].

This means that when a technological paradigm is established the technological community will follow some rules to address and solve problems. For instance in the development of CPUs, it is well know the Moore's law that says that the capacity of the CPU will double every 18 months. This "rule" is both a target for the industry and a strong orientation to solve the relevant problem. In other words all the technologists of the industry are focused to address the improvement of CPU and not other possible dimension of improvements. This paradigm, as explained by Dosi [4], drives innovation and allows predicting the direction of innovation[1].

Using a metaphor, paradigms are "the glasses" of the technological community and tell them what are the relevant problems to address. Understanding "the glasses" of each technological community allows to read the future and anticipate industry evolution.

2.2 Externalities

The diffusion of innovation is enhanced by the availability of externalities.

In economics terms, an externality is defined as an impact on any party that is not directly involved in an economic decision. An externality occurs when an economic activity causes external costs or external benefits to third party stakeholders who did not directly affect the economic transaction. We can have positive or negative externalities. For instance the creation of technical knowledge in a certain field is a positive externality because it facilitates the further development of additional technical knowledge or innovation.

For the technical progress we consider 2 useful examples.

1. Network externalities. An individual buying a product that is interconnected in a network (e.g. a video cellular phone) will increase the usefulness of such phones to

---

[1] Of course the technological paradigm can forecast the direction of the innovation, but not the specific innovation that will allow meeting the goal set by the paradigm.

other people who have a video cellular phone. When each new user of a product increases the value of the same product owned by others, the phenomenon is called a network externality or a network effect.

2. Spillover effects for technical knowledge. Knowledge spillover of inventions and technical information - once an invention (or most other forms of practical information) is discovered or made more easily accessible, others benefit by exploiting the invention or information. For instance the development of knowledge on the best wing profiles according to speed helped the aviation industry to rely on those profiles for aircraft design.

In particular on the aspect of technical knowledge technological change literature has widely recognized that the most important knowledge required for innovation is the tacit knowledge. Tacit knowledge is the type of information and competence that is specific to a certain domain of application (e.g. Ka-multi spot satellite design not general satellite design) and is not easy to transfer from one field to another. Tacit knowledge is seen in contrast to the scientific knowledge that can be applied to many fields and it is more general in its domain of application. The availability of tacit knowledge in a specific industry, typically coming from experience, is a positive externality, because it is a catalyst for innovation.

Positive externalities typically reinforce/accelerate the existing technological trajectory.

3   Satellite Broadband for Consumer: An Interpretation

The broadband satellite for consumer is an illustrative example for the analysis of technological progress because it permits to capture all these forces at work. The satellite industry in fact is the high-technology field that is behind some of the most important innovations of our times, such as satellite television, navigation system, GPS.

The most recent development is the satellite broadband system for consumers that have been developed widely in the US. In 2008 in the US there were almost a million consumers that are using satellite broadband as their primary internet connection [9].

To bring satellite broadband to consumer a certain number of technological components are necessary: (a) the satellite capacity from a geostationary satellite, (b) the end user equipment (antenna and modem), (c) the on-ground equipment (e.g. hubs), (d) other infrastructure (e.g. network, fiber connectivity). Each of these components is developed by a different industry and all together they represent a technological system. The innovation of each component is independent and managed by different actors. For instance satellite is developed by the space industry, while the antenna and the modem are developed by specialized manufactures of electronics/mechanical equipment.

3.1   Recognized Reverse-Salient Points by the Satellite Industry

As we have seen in the previous chapters, in the technological/research community the focus of technologists and engineers is normally concentrated on the recognized

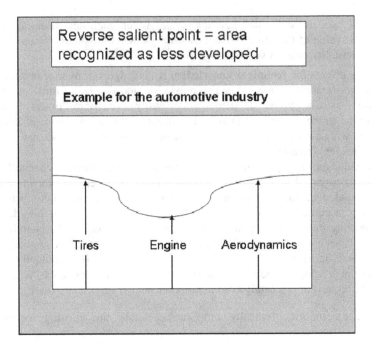

Fig. 1. Example of reverse-salient point for a complex system

critical problems, following the well know concept of paradigm for technological revolutions [5].

New satellite systems for broadband (i.e. the satellite, the end user equipment, the on-ground systems and related infrastructure) are complex system on which each component develops at different speed.

In complex technological systems with several components the effort is concentrated in the area that is perceived to lead to highest improvement. This concept is called reverse-salient from military strategy applied to innovation [6].

In simple terms this means as in the disposition of the military forces the reverse salient is the area less developed, where our army is less advanced (see example above).

During the previous phase the industry concentrated mainly on the reduction of the end-user equipment. The VSAT were initially very expensive around 10.000 US dollars per unit with big antennas. Then, they decreased to 2.000 US dollars thanks to the use of star network architecture with big antennas and the intelligence to share the capacity in the hubs. More recently in 2003 the prices had another decrease below 1.000 US dollars with DVB RCS like systems. The use of standards (such as DOCSIS for ViaSat) and the re-engineering of terminal allowed another dramatic reduction to below 500 dollars.

3.2 The New Reverse Salient: The Satellite Capacity

With price reduction, the industry moved the recognized reversed-salient point. The newly recognized critical problem to address was satellite capacity.

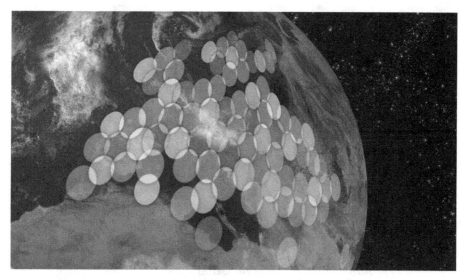

Fig. 2. Eutelsat KA-SAT coverage shows the frequency reuse (different colors for different frequencies)

The industry addressed this problem with spot beams and frequency reuse among the spots with Ka-band frequency with an extraordinary efficacy. The newly designed satellites announced worldwide are those ordered by Eutelsat and ViaSat in Ka-band.

They have made major improvement compared to previous generation thanks to frequency reuse.

Each satellite has specific radio spectrum assigned by regulatory authorities. Each satellite can operate only within that range. The spot beam design of KA-SAT (see figure below) allows a very high "reuse" of the same frequency assignment multiple times on a satellite where each beam of the same colour (i.e. blue, yellow, tan or orange in the below example) broadcasts on the same frequency. Beams of the same colour never touch each other, therefore do not cause interference, and this design allows for much, much greater throughput capacity on the satellite.

The increase of the capacity is supported in two ways by the frequency reuse. On one hand there is an increase of capacity for the reuse of frequency as said before, on the other hand, the reuse allows smaller spots and therefore concentration of power, thus better uplink and downlink performances in the said spots.

Given the complexity of the frequency reuse, the on-ground infrastructure should follow the satellite design to match antennas with spots of the right color, therefore an integrated infrastructural project (satellite + on ground) is needed.

3.3 Dramatic Improve in Performances

The increase in the capacity is dramatic compared to standard Ku-based large beam satellites and to typical Ka-band satellites. We talk about an increase of 18-25 times of available capacity.

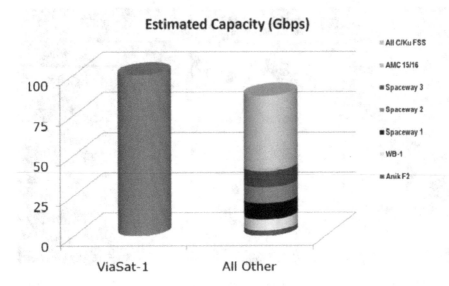

Fig. 3. Analysis of satellite capacity of satellite systems covering the United States

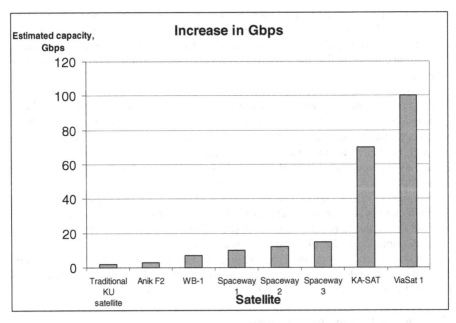

Fig. 4. A dramatic increase of capacity from a satellite of the new generation compared to previous ones (source: industry estimations)

For instance ViaSat-1 satellite in 2011 will have more capacity than the combined C-band, Ku-band and Ka-band satellite now existing in the US (see next chart). From the previous paragraph, we have learned that the main drivers of this improvement are: a) smaller spots that leads on one hand to the increase reuse of frequency and on the other to better coverage (both in uplink and in downlink), c) integrated design of on-ground infrastructure and satellite system.

A deeper analysis of the date of design of the satellite system and the capacity available in Giga-bit per second lead us to believe that a technological trajectory exists, similar to law's Moore for CPU capacity in transistors.

Other operators planning new satellite in the US for broadband use such as Hughes and other companies in Europe and in other Regions seem to go on the same direction, thus confirming the validity of the innovation and the existence of this paradigm.

3.4 The New Paradigm: What Are the New Rules of the Game

If we try to analyze the change from the paradigm perspective, we can better understand this shift in the industry.

The initial paradigm was to make some entry-level service with limited capacity in Ku, we call it *market entry*. The new paradigm is to create a *bit factory*. In the *market entry* the goal was to pursue the most profitable part of the market: business to business market and specialized applications. In the *bit factory* approach the goal is to serve also the consumer market that requires typically more capacity at lower price, but of course they provide a much higher volume of revenues.

We would like to stress especially three new rules of the new paradigm.

1. **Higher chip to enter into this business.** While in the previous paradigm a generic satellite capacity could be used, the new one requires a specifically built satellite or at least a dedicated part of the payload. Given the cost of investing in satellite infrastructure, this raise the stakes for players that want be in the game.

2. **New generation Ka-band satellites need an integrated on-ground infrastructure.** The vision here is to have a global infrastructure both satellite and ground. As we said before given the complexity of the frequency reuse, the on-ground infrastructure should follow the satellite design, therefore an integrated infrastructure is needed.

3. **Higher number of users managed.** The move to consumer and with much more capacity available implies that each operator will have to address a much bigger number of subscribers. This implies the need for proven systems that can manage all these users. This means a concentration of existing hardware vendors.

4. **Closer ties between hardware manufactures and satellite operators.** The importance of ground segment from the satellite development to the operation will drive to closer links within the industry between hardware manufactures and satellite operators.

Table 1. Difference between the 2 paradigms and key dimensions

Paradigm key dimensions	Market entry approach	Bit factory approach
Definition of the technological system	Hub, end-user equipment	Hub, end-user equipment, satellite system
Technological objective	Low terminal price and efficiency in use of capacity	Increase of an order of magnitude the capacity transmitted per unit of cost
Engineering of the solution	Engineering of hub and terminal solution with generic satellite capacity	Integrated engineering of satellite, ground segment and end user equipment
Role of hardware vendor	Off the shelf solution for generic satellite capacity	Customized engineering based on satellite capacity
Importance of hardware manufacturer in satellite design	Not relevant	Relevant throughout the product cycle.
Barrier to entry	Low (few million USD) for antenna and hub equipment	High (require a specific satellite investment)
Risk	Low (investment just on ground)	High (satellite design is not changeable)
Potential clients	Enterprise market, institutions	Consumer market, Enterprise market, institutions
Average number subscriber managed per hub	4-6.000 per hub	Up to 200.000 per hub

3.5 Why Ka-Band

Several reasons explain the choice to go to manufacture a dedicated Ka-band satellite for broadband services [12]:

1. **More spectrum available and better interference environment.** There is more exclusive spectrum available at Ka-band. The Exclusive Band in Ku-band is limited to 250 MHz on the uplink and spans from 14.25 GHz to 14.50 GHz while the available spectrum at Ka-band is double that spectrum, i.e. 500 MHz on both uplink (29.5 – 30GHz) and downlink (19.7 – 20.2GHz). The Exclusive Band in

Ka-band has a better interference environment and its use is limited to small terminals.

2. **Smaller embarked satellite antennas.** Ka-band allows to have smaller antennas on the satellite to cover a spot of a set dimension compared to Ku-band. We assume that the satellite antenna aperture is limited by the satellite configuration and the launch vehicle fairing and that the terminal aperture is defined by the service.

3. **Suitable service availability.** It can be shown that in Europe, for an availability of up to 99.7%, it is still more suitable to work in Ka-band with respect to a Ku-band system.

4. **Ka-band support smaller cells and higher frequency reuse and coverage.** Ka-band is approximately two times higher in frequency than Ku-band. Higher frequency also means that for a given satellite antenna aperture the beam is smaller, allowing smaller cells. Smaller cells imply a better individual coverage.
   On the Forward Link (gateway-to-terminals) this permits to ensure that the satellite power is used efficiently on a more limited area with the required EIRP (effective isotropic radiated power) to get closer to the given user.
   On the Return Link (terminals-to-gateway), this improves the G/T (gain-over-temperature) of the satellite ensuring that for a given bit rate smaller resources are required at the terminals in terms of RF (radio frequency) power required from the HPA (high power amplifier) and antenna aperture. All this contributes towards smaller terminals.

5. **Does not use the commercially valuable DTH frequency.** Using a traditional Ku-band satellite at a premium orbital slot dedicated to DTH services would and reduce capacity for DTH channels.

4 Foreseen Industry Evolution

The future evolution of course depends heavily on the commercial success and profitability of the newly launched satellite broadband projects and on the market opportunity for broadband applications. The well-documented and recognized digital divide in all the countries shows the need for broadband connectivity both in the US and in Europe and seems to fully justify the investment made by the industry [10, 11].

Most recent research study indicates that users will have an increasingly appetite for bandwidth pushing further the logic of the *bit factory* approach versus the logic of *market entry* approach.

In this context old players will have to decide whether they should compete with the old weapons or to invest in the new generation satellite systems completely dedicated to broadband.

The quantum leap of the new paradigm is on one hand too important and on the other too relevant for the service quality not to consider it. Firstly the improvement is too important dimensionally to be neglected (see chart below). Secondly the cost of capacity is so crucial in the service delivery chain that cannot be ignored. We are not talking here about an ancillary feature, but about the single most important reason why customer buy a broadband service, the bandwidth.

Beaming Down
Cost of building satellite
Internet service, per bit

Company	Cost
ViaSat*	$3.50
Eutelsat*	5.00
WildBlue	40.00
SpaceWay*	40.00
Traditional fixed-satellite systems	225.00

* Proposed
Sources: ViaSat and industry estimates

Fig. 5. Cost per Kbps with the new generation of satellites [1]

4.1 Future Ka-Band Applications

The dramatic decrease of industrial cost of satellite capacity might fuel an increase number of applications based on Ka-band.

On the broadband business besides typical broadband access the additional applications are: VOIP, IPTV, and other Ku/Ka DTH video service. Players are moving towards a stronger push for triple play service where the DTH in Ku can be seen an additional video service on top of IPTV. This is why Eutelsat in Europe is talking about 3+1 services (triple play on Ka and video on Ku).

On broadcasting area the main applications are: personal broadcasting, regional television on satellite, micro-broadcasting, and also satellite news gathering to support smaller players. All these application will benefit from the lower cost of capacity and the regional coverage of spot beams.

On the data business key applications are: business to business applications, high-speed data casting (with peak speed above 100 Mbps), back-up for emergencies. These applications are supported by the much higher capability of the satellite and the new technology available.

With the success of these applications the *bit-factory approach* might be pushed further. Again the application development is another of the key positive externality that has a strong network effect and can lead to exponential adoption rates. All these elements create the demand for Ka-band and will push for even bigger capacity satellites.

4.2 Ka-Band: A Bright Future Ahead

Externalities will play an important role in making stronger the future of Ka-Band.

The important investment already done by WildBlue, ViaSat and Eutelsat in the most advanced markets for broadband can have positive spillover effects on technical knowledge both the competence required for the mass production of antennas, hardware, and other RF components (both in the hubs and in the end-user equipment) and on the industry competence to produce satellite. Of these competences some of this is strictly related to Ka-band (like the RF part and the satellite skills on Ka), the other is somehow transferable to Ku. Only the first one will play a major role in supporting the choice of Ka-band.

Moreover new applications like regional television that have strong network effects can drive adoption of Ka-band end-user equipment in larger areas of the population in Europe as in happens in the US.

Both effects will reinforce the choice of Ka-band in the future for these type of systems in Western Europe and North America.

5 Conclusions

In the interpretation of the technological evolution of the satellite broadband industry, this paper shows that the reverse-salient points moved from cost of the end user terminal to the satellite capacity.

The paradigm has moved from a *market entry* approach to a *bit factory* approach. This implies a) a closer activity between hardware manufactures and satellite operators in the satellite broadband market; b) a higher concentration of the industry both on the hardware vendors and on the service operators at least for Ka-band segment; c) more integrated design of satellite and on ground segment.

We foresee that there is a technological trajectory in this area, similar to Moore's law in the computer industry driving down the cost of capacity.

We argue that there will be a bigger role for Ka-band systems in the future thanks to the positive externalities that the investment of 3 major companies have done so far and will do in this market. Ka-band for satellite broadband seems here to stay.

References

1. Pasztor, A.: Firms Team Up to Offer Internet Via Satellite in Trans-Atlantic Push. Wall Street Journal, A16 (January 8, 2008)
2. NSR, Crystal Balling the Transformed World of Ka-Band Broadband Services, Broadband satellite markets, 6th edn. (2008)
3. Rosenberg, N.: Inside the Black Box: Technology and Economics. Cambridge University Press, Cambridge (1982)
4. Dosi, G.: Technological paradigms and technological trajectories: A suggested interpretation of the determinants and directions of technical change, Research Policy, Elsevier 11(3), 147–162 (1982)
5. Vincenti, W.G.: What Engineers Know and how They Know it: Analytical Studies from Aeronautical History. Johns Hopkins University Press, Baltimore (1990)
6. Soutaris, V.: Technological trajectories as moderators of firm-level determinants of innovation. Research Policy 31(6), 877–898 (2002)

7. Kuhn, T.S.: The Structure of Scientific Revolutions. University of Chicago, Chicago (1970)
8. Hughes, T.P.: Reverse salients and critical problems: the dynamics of technological change. In: Dosi, G., Giannetti, R., Toninelli, P.A. (eds.) Technology and enterprise in a historical perspective, pp. 97–118. Clarendon Press, Oxford (1987)
9. NSR, Broadband satellite markets, 6th edn., pp. 1–6 (2008)
10. iDate, Satellite Broadband in Europe & North Africa (April 2008)
11. United States Government Accountability Office, GAO, Report to Congressional Commitees, Telecommunications, Broadband Deployment (May 2006)
12. Benoit, G., Fenech, H., Pezzana, S.: Triple play over satellite, Ka-band making the difference. In: International Conference on Personal Satellite Services, PSATS 2009, Draft version (March 2009)

Performance Enhanced Proxy Solutions for Satellite Networks: State of the Art, Protocol Stack and Possible Interfaces

Igor Bisio, Mario Marchese, and Maurizio Mongelli

Abstract. There are many types of *Performance Enhancing Proxies* (PEPs). Different types of PEPs are used in different environments to overcome different link characteristics which affect protocol performance [1]. The main examples concerns satellite and wireless networks, which represent the most challenging environments.

In the following, the main concepts representing the state of the art of the PEP will be introduced. An extension to the ETSI *Broadband Satellite Multimedia* (BSM) is proposed, in order to include PEP interfaces.

1 Introduction

There are many types of Performance Enhancing Proxies (PEPs). Different types of PEPs are used in different environments to overcome different link characteristics which affect protocol performance [1]. The main examples concerns satellite and wireless networks, which represent the most challenging environments. More specifically, PEPs are network agents designed to improve the end-to-end performance of some communications protocol such as Transmission Control Protocol. PEPs function by breaking the end-to-end connection into multiple connections and using different parameters to transfer data across the different legs. This allows the end systems to run unmodified and can overcome some problems with TCP window sizes on the end systems being set too low for satellite communications. A typical system uses transport layer PEPs to improve TCP performance over a satellite link. The end systems use standard TCP with no modifications, and do not need to know of the existence of the PEPs in between. The transport layer PEPs intercept the TCP connections from the end systems and terminate them. The PEPs then use some other protocol to transfer data between them before translating back to TCP to send the data to the destination.

2 Types of PEPs

a) Transport Layer PEPs
Transport layer PEPs operate at the transport level. They may be aware of the type of application being carried by the transport layer but, at most, only use this information to influence their behavior with respect to the transport protocol; they do not modify the application protocol in any way, but let the application protocol operate end-to-end.

K. Sithamparanathan (Ed.): Psats 2009, LNICST 15, pp. 61–67, 2009.

b) Application Layer PEPs

Some application protocols employ extraneous round trips, overly verbose headers and/or inefficient header encoding which may have a significant impact on performance, in particular, with long delay and slow satellite links. This unnecessary overhead can be reduced, in general or for a particular type of link, by using an application layer PEP in an intermediate node.

3 PEPs' Implementations

Another important characteristic of PEPs concerns the Distribution. A PEP implementation may be integrated (i.e., it comprises a single PEP component implemented within a single node), or distributed (i.e., it comprises two or more PEP components, typically implemented in multiple nodes). An integrated PEP implementation represents a single point at which performance enhancement is applied. A distributed PEP implementation is generally used to surround a particular link for which performance enhancement is desired. For example, a PEP implementation for a satellite connection may be distributed between two PEPs located at each end of the satellite link. A typical example of a distributed PEP is the Satlabs I-PEP [2] and an example of integrated PEP is the PEPsal solution [3].

a) Split Connections Concept

A very important role in PEP architecture is played by the split connection TCP implementation. It terminates the TCP connection received from an end system and establishes a corresponding TCP connection to the other end system. In a distributed PEP implementation, this is typically done to allow the use of a third connection between two PEPs optimized for the link (for example the I-PEP protocol that is recommended by Satlabs).

4 Overview of PEP Mechanisms

An obvious key characteristic of a PEP implementation is the mechanism(s) it uses to improve performance. Some examples of PEP mechanisms are described in the following subsections. A PEP implementation might implement more than one of these mechanisms:

❖ TCP ACK Handling: many TCP PEP implementations are based on TCP ACK manipulation. The handling of TCP acknowledgments can differ significantly between different TCP PEP implementations.

❖ TCP ACK Spacing: in environments where ACKs tend to bunch together, ACK spacing is used to smooth out the flow of TCP acknowledgments traversing a link.

❖ Local TCP Acknowledgements: in some PEP implementations, TCP data segments received by the PEP are locally acknowledged by the PEP.

❖ Local TCP Retransmissions: a TCP PEP may locally retransmit data segments lost on the path between the TCP PEP and the receiving end system, thus aiming at faster recovery from lost data.

❖ TCP ACK Filtering and Reconstruction: on paths with highly asymmetric bandwidth the TCP ACKs flowing in the low-speed direction may get congested if the asymmetry ratio is high enough.

Other important functionalities may play important role in the overall PEP action. In more detail, they are:

a) Tunnelling

A Performance Enhancing Proxy may encapsulate messages in a tunnel to carry the messages across a particular link or to force messages to traverse a particular path. A PEP at the other end of the encapsulation tunnel removes the tunnel wrappers before final delivery to the receiving end system.

b) Compression

Many PEP implementations include support for one or more forms of compression. In some PEP implementations, compression may even be the only mechanism used for performance improvement.

c) Handling Periods of Link Disconnection with TCP

During link disconnection or link outage periods, a TCP sender does not receive the expected acknowledgments. Upon expiration of the retransmit timer, this causes TCP to close its congestion window with all of the related drawbacks.

d) Priority-based Multiplexing

Implementing priority-based multiplexing of data over a slow and expensive link may significantly improve the performance and usability of the link for selected applications or connections. A user behind a slow link would experience the link more feasible to use in case of simultaneous data transfers, if urgent data transfers (e.g., interactive connections) could have shorter response time (better performance) than less urgent background transfers. If the interactive connections transmit enough data to keep the slow link fully utilized, it might be necessary to fully suspend the background transfers for awhile to ensure timely delivery for the interactive connections.

5 PEP Protocol Stack

In Fig. 1, the PEP node functional architecture has been reported [4]. The node owns a specific application layer employed to manage the needed functions of the PEP. The functionalities of each individuated layer have been listed in the following by considering the PEP node acting together with the Satellite Terminal (ST) node. In practice, as previously said, the ST nodes operates as QoS Gateway (GW) and the PEP node implements all the functions aimed at optimizing the end-to-end data transfers based on the TCP.

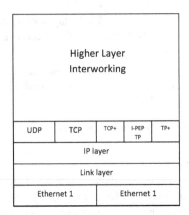

Fig. 1. General PEP protocol architecture

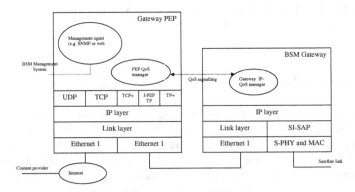

Fig. 2. BSM ST PEP

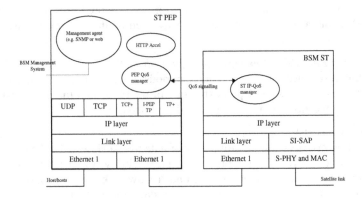

Fig. 3. BSM Gateway PEP

Figs. 2 and 3 show the ST and GW combined with PEP protocol architectures respectively. On the satellite network sides, the ST/GW PEP are connected to BSM ST/GW through an Ethernet LAN. However, the GW PEP can be located remotely from the BSM GW terminal (such as GW PEP run by a service provider). The transport protocol in the PEP is divided between standard TCP/UDP and PEP specific transport protocols. The PEP specific transport protocol can be as follows. A modified TCP (TCP+), such as TCP Hybla, which is used in integrated PEP configurations, where only GW PEP will be used (no ST PEP). Standards I-PEP transport protocol (I-PEP TP [2]) is recommended for distributed PEP configurations.

6 PEP and ST/BSM Nodes' Interfaces

The ETSI-TS102292 and ETSI-TR101984 standards define the internal and external interfaces of the BSM architecture. In this section, their approach is generalized to the presence of PEP devices, coherently with the protocol architecture envisaged in last section. The interfaces including PEP are depicted in Fig. 4. The reference topology is the star one, where ST sends/recieves packets to/from the GW of the network. The case of mesh topology is in coherence with the proposed solution, too.

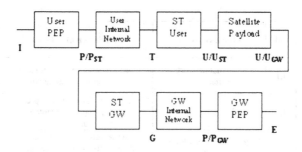

Fig. 4. Reference model of BSM with PEP access

The corresponding description is reported in following table. The Internal network considered regards any possible connection used to link the PEP node to the ST/BSM node.

Fig. 5 deals with the reference model of the BSM architecture together with PEP node interfaces. The following table details all the named interfaces of Fig. 5. Interfaces between I.10 and I.16 (right side of Fig. 5) are specular to interfaces I.1-I.7, the only difference relies on referring to GW PEP device in place of ST PEP device (left side of Fig. 5).

Ref.	Physical Interface Name	Description of Interface
I	User PEP/ External Network Interface	Interface between user PEP and premises network
P/P$_{ST}$	PEP/User Internal Network inteface	Interface between PEP node on user side and internal network
T	ST/Internal Network Inteface	Interface between User ST and Internal Interface
U/U$_{ST}$	ST/Satellite Network Interface	Satellite Radio Interface for User ST
U/U$_{GW}$	ST/Satellite Network Interface	Satellite Radio Interface for Gateway
G	ST/ Internal Network Interface	Interface between Gateway ST and internal network
P/P$_{GW}$	PEP/ Internal Network Interface	Interface between Gateway PEP and internal network
E	PEP/ External Network Interface	Interface between Gateway PEP and external network

Ref.	Interface Name	Description of Interface
I.1	External network interface	Interface between end system and customer premises network
I.2	PEP ST interface	External interface between premises network and PEP adaptation function
I.3	PEP ST Technology Independent interface	Internal interface between PEP adaptation function and Technology Independent layer
I.4	PEP ST Technology Dependent interface	Internal interface between Technology Independent layer and Technology Dependent layer
I.5	ST interface	External interface between PEP Technology Dependent layer and satellite access function
I.6	BSM subnetwork service access point	Internal interface
I.7	BSM satellite independent service access point SI-SAP	Internal interface

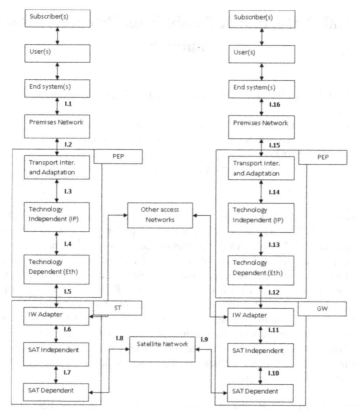

Fig. 5. PEP node Interfaces

7   Conclusions

The paper has presented most important aspectsconcerning the Performance Enhancing Proxies (PEPs), suited to be used over satellite channel. These indication may represent a useful set of suggestions to design, realize and test a real PEP system in future Quality of Service oriented satellite networks. Specific attention has been devoted to include PEP interface in the ETSI Broadband Satellite Multimedia (BSM) standards.

References

[1] IETF RFC 3135: Performance Enhancing Proxies Intended to Mitigate Link-Related Degradations
[2] I-PEP specifications, Issue 1a. Satlabs group recommendations (October 2005), http://www.satlabs.org
[3] Caini, C., Firrincieli, R., Lacamera, D.: PEPsal: a Performance Enhancing Proxy designed for TCP satellite connections. In: IEEE 63rd Vehicular Technology Conference, 2006. VTC 2006-Spring, May 2006, vol. 6, pp. 2607–2611 (2006)
[4] Cruickshank, H., Mort, R., Berioli, M.: PEP Architecture for Broadband Satellite Multimedia (BSM) Networks. In: Workshop on Satellite PEPs Current Status and Future Directions, Nordwijk, The Netherlands (December 2, 2008)

PEPsal Performance Analysis on Disruptive Radio Channels

Carlo Caini[1], Rosario Firrincieli[1], and Daniele Lacamera[2]

[1] DEIS dep., University of Bologna, Bologna, Italy
[2] SADEL S.p.A., Castel Maggiore, Bologna, Italy
{ccaini,rfirrincieli}@arces.unibo.it
root@danielinux.net

Abstract. Fixed GEO satellite communications are impaired by long RTTs (especially GEO) and the possible presence of packet losses on the satellite radio channels. Moreover, when the satellite receiver is mobile, short and long disruptions due to line of sight obstructions associated with the presence of shadowing can cause further performance deterioration. In this paper, we evaluate the impact of a disruptive channel on PEPsal, a TCP-splitting PEP previously developed by the authors. Results, obtained by emulating the satellite link interruptions caused by tunnels of a real railway line, highlight the advantages of the TCP-splitting architecture. By enabling the adoption of optimized version of TCP on the satellite connection and a satellite-specific tuning of TCP parameters, PEPsal can offer a significant resilience against all kind of satellite impairments.

Keywords: PEP, TCP, disruptive channels, satellite communications, trains, testbed.

1 Introduction

Fixed GEO satellite communications are impaired by long RTTs (especially GEO) and the possible presence of packet losses on the satellite radio channels [1]. The channel is generally available, except for limited amounts of time when the system may go in outage due to particularly severe additional attenuations. However, when the satellite receiver is mobile, short and long disruptions due to line of sight obstructions associated with the presence of shadowing can cause further significant performance deteriorations.

The aim of this paper is to investigate the impact of disruptions on end-to-end TCP connections and PEP architectures [2], focusing in particular on PEPsal, a free software implementation of the TCP-splitting concept, developed by the authors [3], [4]. To this end, the algorithm of TCP RTO (Retransmission Time Out) timer [5], [6], whose role is essential in presence of disruptions, is briefly reviewed, by pointing out both RFC indications and Linux implementation. RTO is usually doubled by TCP at each unsuccessful retransmission, following the so called "exponential backoff algorithm". This conservative policy is justified if losses are caused by congestion, in order to preserve the stability of the network. However, in presence of long

K. Sithamparanathan (Ed.): Psats 2009, LNICST 15, pp. 68–76, 2009.

disruptions, this technique may introduce a long unjustified delay between the end of a channel disconnection and the consequent retransmission restart. RFC 1122 [6] considers as an optional feature the possibility of restricting the exponential growth of RTO, by setting a maximum RTO value (not lower, however, than 60 s, for the same stability concerns as before). Linux exploits this feature by setting the maximum RTO to 120 s by default in the kernel code. As shown in the paper, this feature plays an important role in limiting the restart delay. For this reason, the default Linux value is changed, to study the impact on performance. In particular, also values lower than 60 s, although not strictly RFC compliant, are considered in the PEP node only, by taking advantage of the isolation of the satellite link from the rest of the network granted by the TCP-splitting PEP.

As a practical case study, we consider disruptions caused by railway tunnels, focusing in particular on one of the most important Italian railways lines, the Bologna-Florence "Direttissima". Performance is evaluated by means of the Linux based TATPA (Testbed on Advanced Transport Protocols and Architectures) testbed [7], [8]. To the usual performance evaluation tools present in TATPA, a new module has been added to emulate disruptions on the satellite channel.

A series of test has been carried out to compare PEPsal and standard end-to-end TCP performance in presence of disruptions, to evaluate the impact of the train speed and that of the maximum RTO. Results are widely discussed in the last section of the paper.

2   TCP Timers

From the TCP perspective, a disruptive channel poses serious constraints to the end-to-end performance. The TCP connection is ruled by four main timers [5], [6] and [9]: the *retransmission timer*, the *keep alive* timer, the *2MSL* and the *persist* timers. Concerning disruptions, the first one has the greatest impact; therefore we will focus our attention on it in the rest of the paper.

2.1   The Retransmission Timer Algorithm

TCP is a reliable transmission protocol that requires positive acknowledgments of transmitted data. It uses the retransmission timer to react to a possible feedback absence from the remote data receiver. The duration of this timer is referred to as RTO (Retransmission Time Out). During the connection lifetime the current RTO, is computed from two estimated variables, SRTT (Smoothed RTT) and RTTVAR (RTT Variation). Details on how RTO is actually computed starting from these variables can be found in [6]. After the first RTO expiring, the last unacknowledged segment is retransmitted and the initial RTO value is doubled, by following the so called *exponential backoff* mechanism, and so on in case of successive RTO expirations, a case that may be easily triggered by disruptions. Before examining in details the RTO algorithm, let us recall the limits posed to the possible RTO values by RFC2988 [6]. It first states that RTO should be conservatively rounded up at 1 s to avoid spurious timeouts. It is worth noting that Linux OS implementation, however, fixes this minimum value to a lower threshold (TCP_RTO_MIN = 200 ms), perhaps because it can relies on a fine clock grain (1 ms) and on advanced spurious timeouts recognition techniques, such as F-RTO [10]. The same RFC states that also a maximum RTO value may be optionally set. In this case, its value must be at least 60 s.

The TCP retransmission algorithm is quite complex to describe as it consists of many mandatory and optional features, which leave space to multiple implementations.

We can distinguish between two algorithm phases: before and after the RTO expiration. In the former case, the TCP sender applies the following actions [6]:

1.   every time a packet containing data is sent (including a retransmission), if the timer is not running, it is started so that it will expire after RTO seconds (for the current value of RTO);
2.   when all outstanding data has been acknowledged, the retransmission timer is turned off;
3.   when an ACK is received that acknowledges new data, the retransmission timer is restarted so that it will expire after RTO seconds (for the current value of RTO).

Then, after the RTO expiration, we have the following steps:

1.   the earliest segment that has not been acknowledged by the TCP receiver is retransmitted;
2.   the TCP sender backs off the RTO by doubling it $(RTO = 2\,RTO)$. A maximum value may be applied to provide a ceiling to this doubling operation; as aforementioned, this optional feature is adopted in Linux $(TCP\_RTO\_MAX = 120\,s)$;
3.   the retransmission timer is started, such that it expires after RTO seconds (for the value of RTO after the doubling operation);
4.   if the retransmission timer expires again for the same packet, the RTO is further doubled, the timer is restarted and the segment is retransmitted;
5.   In [5] it is stated that the previous point must be repeated either for a given time or for a given number of retries; in Linux the choice is to set a threshold on the number of retries (TCP_RETR2 variable). After this threshold is reached, and the transmission of the segment still fails, the connection is closed. There is also a lower threshold (TCP_RETR1 variable) which allows the TCP to pass negative advice to the IP layer, which in turn triggers dead-gateway diagnosis. Linux default values for these variables are respectively: TCP_RETR1 = 3 and TCP_RETR2 = 15.

2.2   Remarks on the Maximum Tolerable Disruption Length, and TCP Agility on Restarting Transmission

The Linux choice in favor of retries threshold, implies that the maximum tolerable disruption length (i.e. that does not cause the connection closing) is not directly set, but depends on the RTO value at disruption start, the number of allowed retries (TCP_RETR2) and the max RTO (TCP_RTO_MAX). It is worth stressing the role played by this last parameter in both determining the maximum tolerable disruption length and the "agility" of TCP to restart transmission after relatively long disruptions. Actually, in the presence of a long disruption the channel availability is probed at doubling time intervals until the maximum RTO value is reached. Then, it is probed at constant regular intervals until the maximum number of retransmission is reached. As the maximum RTO value represents the maximum time interval between a channel probe and the following, it also represents the worst case for the delay between a disruption end and the subsequent transmission restart. Moreover, if we assume disruption lengths uniformly distributed between two consecutive probes, the average restart delay is upper bounded by half the maximum RTO (first retransmissions are actually faster). The longer this delay, the higher the penalization in performance, as the channel is left unexploited fro more time.

In conclusions, the maximum RTO value represents the worst case delay before retransmission restart and its half the average delay for last retransmissions, when RTO has already reached its maximum value. The higher the maximum RTO threshold, the higher the restart delays. On the other hand, for a given maximum number of retries, the higher the maximum RTO, the longer the maximum tolerable disruption. In the following we exploit the possibility of tuning TCP_RTO_MAX and TCP_RETR2 variables to improve TCP agility while maintaining the maximum tolerable disruption length. To this regard we modified the Linux kernel in order to make the TCP_RTO_MAX variable accessible by the sysctl tool.

3 PEPsal

The category of Performance Enhancing Proxies (PEPs) embraces a wide variety of different techniques operating at different levels, as clearly shown in [2]. In brief, PEPsal [3] can be described as a TCP accelerator based on the TCP-splitting technique, implemented in Linux and made freely available [4] under the GPL license. Following the RFC classification PEPsal is a "multi-layer" proxy, because in order to implement the TCP splitting technique, it must operate at Network, Transport and Application layers. PEPsal can be classified as "integrated", since it runs only on a single box on the forward link satellite gateway. It is worth noting that this characteristic differentiates it by most of commercial PEPs based on the same TCP-splitting techniques, which, by contrast, are usually "distributed", running on two boxes at both ends of the satellite link. In the usual configuration PEPsal is "asymmetric", i.e. it is active only in the forward direction (from the satellite gateway to the end user), but it can be made easily "symmetric" (i.e. active in both forward and return directions) just by introducing a few modifications on the receiver side. Finally, PEPsal is "transparent" to the users in the customary asymmetric configuration, as TCP users are unaware of the connection splitting performed at the intermediate satellite gateway.

The PEPsal architecture is shown in Figure 1. The end-to-end TCP connection is split into a pair of separated connections, with the aim of isolating the satellite channel. On the first connection, from the TCP server to the satellite gateway, it is adopted a standard TCP variant, like NewReno. By contrast, on the second, from the satellite gateway to the TCP client, it is definitively better to adopt an enhanced TCP variant, to better cope with long RTTs and the possible presence of segment losses due to residual bit errors on the satellite link. The suggested choice is TCP Hybla [11], a TCP variant specifically designed to cope with the long RTTs typical of satellite channels. However, PEPsal allows all the other TCP variants implemented in

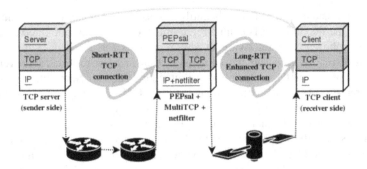

Fig. 1. PEPsal architecture (based on integrated TCP-splitting approach)

Linux (more than ten at present) to be adopted as well. As all of them are compatible with standard TCP clients, both the TCP server and the TCP client can continue to use standard TCP, being actually unaware of the PEPsal presence in the middle.

The splitting of the end-to-end connection in two segments, allows a greater freedom of choice in the setting of TCP timers related to timeout and retransmissions. In fact, being the satellite connection isolated from the network core, it is possible to consider more frequent channel probes of what usually allowed on end-to-end channels, if necessary. This is a possibility that is explored in the paper, by tuning the TCP_RTO_MAX value. In particular, this parameter is reduced from 120 s (the Linux default) to 10 s in order to limit the restart delay after disruption ends. Although not RFC compliant [6], its adoption is safe also from the network point of view, because the more frequent channel probes made through segment retransmissions have a null impact on the open network, being strictly confined on the satellite connection.

4 The TATPA Testbed

The design of TATPA (Testbed on Advanced Transport Protocol and Architectures) [7] aims to reproduce the essential characteristics of heterogeneous networks that include satellite links. Its logical layout (much simpler than the corresponding physical layout based on a cluster of Linux PCs) is depicted in Figure 2. The choice of the Linux platform was dictated by a number of reasons that make it very appealing to the research community: GNU/Linux system is free, fully customizable by the user, and offers the network researcher a wide number of TCP variants already available in the standard OS package. In addition to widely adopted network tools, such as NistNet [12] and Iperf [13], TATPA also exploits some software packages specifically developed by the authors to extend its features (these software tools are also made available to the scientific community under the GNU license). Among them, we cite the Multi TCP package [14], which allows us to include the full version of TCP Hybla [11] and to collect logs of internal variables (like RTO), the PEPsal package, discussed in the previous section, and the reference implementation of Bundle Layer DTN (Delay Tolerant Networks) [15]. Last but not least, in order to emulate satellite channel disruptions, we realized a time-discrete Gilbert-Elliot [16] channel emulator. Such a channel discards all arriving packets when in its bad state,

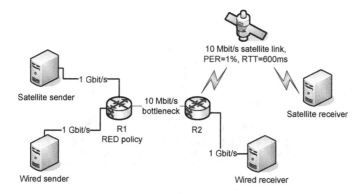

Fig. 2. The TATPA logical layout

while leaves untouched flowing packets when in its good state. In order to determine the good-bad states transitions, both statistical and deterministic trace-based methods have been implemented. In this paper, we exploited the second possibility, by making use of real railways tunnel traces.

5   A Case Study: Disruptions Caused by Railway Tunnels

As mentioned above, disruptive channels can be present when mobility is concerned. Tunnels on railway or highway are a practical significant example of disruptiveness induced by mobility. Here, we will focus on railway tunnels, considering real data referring to one of the most important and significant Italian railways lines.

5.1   The Characteristics of the "Direttissima" Bologna-Florence Railway Line

Bologna is one of the most important railway nodes in Italy. It is located roughly a hundred kilometers North of Florence, from which is separated by the Apennines mount chain. Bologna and Florence are at present connected by two lines, of which one is of local interest only, while the second, called "Direttissima" and considered here, is the most important railway link for both passengers and freight traffic between North and Central Italy. "Direttissima" was opened to the service in 1934. It is about 96 km long and has been chosen not only because of its practical relevance but also because it is characterized by an interesting mix of tunnels of different lengths interlaced with open sky segments. In the whole, there are 33 tunnels on the line, of which the longest is of about 18.5 km, while the average length is of 1.1 km. The whole length of tunnels is of 37 km, equal to 39% of the line. Of course, the longer the tunnel, the longer the corresponding satellite channel disruption, the actual values being dependent on the train speed. Assuming a constant speed of 120 km/h (typical of the average speed of passenger train on the line) we obtain the values given in Figure 3. Value for other speeds can be directly derived from these.

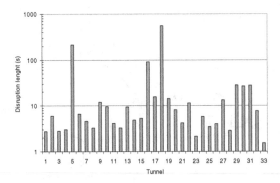

Fig. 3. Bologna-Florence railway line; length of channel disruptions caused by tunnels (train speed=120 km/h)

A new high speed railway line is going to be completed by the end of 2009. It has not been considered here because most of it will be in tunnels, with very short open sky segments.

5.2 Numerical Results

Numerical results, obtained through TATPA, are presented in Figure 4 and Figure 5. They refer to a single satellite connection that lasts for the entire train journey, from Bologna to Florence. Performance is given in terms of final goodput, calculated considering only the clear sky percentage of the connection lifetime (61% in the considered scenario). The objective is to highlight the TCP ability to exploit the channel when it is not disrupted by tunnels. Moreover, we have assumed the link affected by a 1% Packet Error Rate (PER), to take into account possible radio link impairments outside the tunnels. It is worth noting that the tested link is extremely challenging, encompassing at the same time a long RTT (600ms), a high PER (1%) and frequent disruptions (39% of the entire connection lifetime).

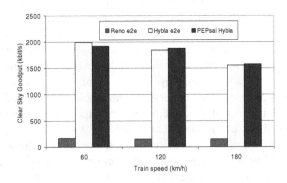

Fig. 4. Comparison between end-to-end TCP and PEPsal; clear sky goodput versus different train speeds

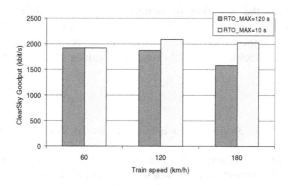

Fig. 5. Impact of TCP_MAX_RTO on PEPsal clear sky goodput for different train speeds

In Figure 4 end-to-end Reno, end-to-end Hybla and PEPsal are compared considering different train speeds (60, 120 and 180 km/h). All of tested protocols and architectures are considered with the default TCP_RTO_MAX, while TCP_RETR2 has been properly increased to cope with the almost 20 minutes disruption caused by the longest tunnel in the 60 km/h case. The outcome confirms the well known Hybla superiority over Reno, when applied in satellite environments. With respect to previous results presented in the literature [3], here the channel is more challenging, being affected, as previously pointed out, not only by a high PER but also by frequent disruptions. PEPsal, using Hybla in its second connection, shows the same performance of end-to-end Hybla, with the great advantage of being transparent also to the sender, which, consequently, does not require to be modified as in the end-to-end approach.

As aforementioned, the splitting nature of PEPsal allows the modification of TCP_RTO_MAX on the second connection without affecting the rest of the network. This important parameter can be reduced to decrease the TCP restart delay after a disruption. However, a reduction of the RTO max value without a correspondent increasing of the maximum number of retransmissions (TCP_RETR2) results in a diminution of the maximum tolerable disruption length. In Figure 5 we focused on PEPsal performance to have a first assessment of the TCP_RTO_MAX impact. To this end we have compared previous results (120 s) with those achievable by reducing TCP_RTO_MAX to just 10 s. In this case we have also further increased the TCP_RETR2 to preserve the maximum tolerable disruption length. Results show that, especially at high train speeds, reducing the RTO max value effectively decreases the restart delay, with a consequent enhancement of the final goodput.

6   Conclusions

In the paper, the performance achievable by a TCP-splitting PEP architecture operating on a GEO satellite link have been analyzed, with particular emphasis on the impact of channel disruptions. Results, obtained by emulating the satellite link interruptions caused by tunnels of a real railway line, highlight the advantages of the TCP-splitting architecture. By isolating the satellite impairments from the rest of the network, it enables the adoption of optimized version of TCP on the satellite connection and a satellite-specific tuning of TCP parameters, like the RTO maximum value investigated in the paper. In this way, a better resilience against all kind of satellite impairments, included channel disruptions, can be easily achieved.

References

1. Hu, Y., Li, V.O.H.: Satellite-based internet: a tutorial. IEEE Commun. Mag. 39(3), 164–171 (2001)
2. Border, J., Kojo, M., Griner, J., Montenegro, G., Shelby, Z.: Performance Enhancing Proxies Intended to Mitigate Link-Related Degradations, IETF RFC 3135 (June 2001)
3. Caini, C., Firrincieli, R., Lacamera, D.: PEPsal: a Performance Enhancing Proxy for TCP satellite connections. IEEE Aerospace and Electronic Systems Magazine 22(8), B–9–B–16 (2007)
4. PEPsal: http://sourceforge.net/projects/pepsal/
5. Braden, R.: Requirements for Internet Hosts—Communication Layers, IETF RFC 1122 (October 1989)
6. Paxon, W., Allman, M.: Computing TCP's Retransmission Timer, IETF RFC 2988 (November 2000)
7. Caini, C., Firrincieli, R., Lacamera, D., Tamagnini, S., Tiraferri, D.: The TATPA Testbed, a Testbed for Advanced Transport Protocols and Architecture performance evaluation on wireless channels. In: Proc. IEEE TridentCom, Orlando, Florida, pp. 1–7 (2007)
8. TATPA website: https://tatpa.deis.unibo.it
9. Stevens, W.R.: TCP/IP Illustrated, vol. 1. Addison-Wesley, Reading (1994)
10. Sarolahti, P., Kojo, M.: Forward RTO-Recovery (F-RTO): An Algorithm for Detecting Spurious Retransmission Timeouts with TCP and the Stream Control Transmission Protocol (SCTP), IETF RFC 4138 (August 2005)
11. Caini, C., Firrincieli, R.: TCP Hybla: a TCP Enhancement for Heterogeneous Networks. Int. J. Satell. Commun. Network 22, 547–566 (2004)
12. NistNet web site: http://snad.ncsl.nist.gov/itg/nistnet/
13. Iperf web site, http://dast.nlanr.net/Projects/Iperf/
14. Caini, C., Firrincieli, R., Lacamera, D.: A Linux Based Multi TCP Implementation for Experimental Evaluation of TCP Enhancements. In: Proc. SPECTS 2005, Philadelphia (July 2005)
15. Cerf, V., Hooke, A., Torgerson, L., Durst, R., Scott, K., Fall, K., Weiss, H.: Delay-Tolerant Networking Architecture, Request for Comment, IETF RFC 4838 (April 2007)
16. Gilbert, E.N.: Capacity of a burst-noise channel. The Bell System Technical Journal 39, 1253–1265 (1960)

PEP Deployment and Bandwidth Management Issues

Charles Younghusband, Peter Slade, and Jeff Weaver

XipLink, Inc.
Suite 800, 3981 boul. St-Laurent, Montréal, QC, Canada H2W 1Y5
{cyounghusband,pslade,jweaver}@xiplink.com

Abstract. This paper will discuss current deployment scenarios for Performance Enhancement Proxies (PEP) technologies in broadband satellite access systems from the perspective of one PEP technology provider. Recent improvements such as DVB-S2 can provide substantial gains at the link layer. In order to achieve further efficiency gains, the satellite industry is now forced to look elsewhere – namely other layers in the data communications network stack. Satellite terminal manufacturers are now moving beyond basic TCP acceleration techniques to more comprehensive optimization techniques that incorporate advances in data compression and flexibility for more deployment scenarios. Some of the advances for PEP technology are in part due to CPU and memory technology advances, resulting in increasingly affordable access to computing power, allowing PEP manufacturers deliver substantial performance and bandwidth savings gains.

1 Introduction

Performance Enhancing Proxies (PEP) are TCP split-connection solutions to address the properties and limitations of wireless communications using various techniques, transparently or non-transparently to the end-hosts, and have been previously addressed by the IETF in RFC 3135 [1]. PEPs can also perform other functions such as compression and application specific optimization. This is of particular relevance to satellite communications given the high cost of bandwidth. They can also be combined with other intermediate-node network technologies such as virtual private networks (VPNs).

This paper will discuss current deployment scenarios for Performance Enhancement Proxies (PEP) technologies in broadband satellite access systems from the perspective of one PEP technology provider. Recent improvements such as DVB-S2 can provide substantial gains at the link layer, and the satellite industry is now forced to look elsewhere – namely other layers in the data communications network stack -- for efficiency gains. Satellite terminal manufacturers are now moving beyond basic TCP acceleration techniques to more comprehensive optimization techniques that incorporate advances in data compression and flexibility for more deployment scenarios. In part this is due to improved PEP technology, but some of the advances for PEP technology are due to CPU and memory technology advances, results in an increasingly affordable access to computing power, allowing PEP manufacturers deliver substantial performance and bandwidth savings gains.

K. Sithamparanathan (Ed.): Psats 2009, LNICST 15, pp. 77–84, 2009.

This allows PEP manufacturers to reduce cost and deliver substantial gains. For instance, very small (pocket-sized) solutions are now available to users to further broaden the deployment availability of advanced PEP and link optimization technology.

A PEP technology provider looking beyond a narrow technology application is also required to examine many different deployment scenarios, not just in the context of a particular satellite networking technology but the topology and impacts of encryption and the possibly use of multiple paths or meshed and hybrid networks. This paper will briefly discuss some issues with deployment scenarios for VSATS and Mobile Satellite Services and bandwidth management issues that arise from the combination of the deployment scenarios with optimization techniques.

This paper assumes basic familiarity with PEPs and other optimization techniques used for satellite and wireless data systems.

2 PEP Technology

Besides the well known TCP Acceleration to address the limitations of standard TCP/IP when used over satellite [2], some of the techniques now being applied to reduce bandwidth demands include compression, filtering of rogue Internet traffic, shaping of traffic, data suppression, optimization of particular application protocols, header compression as well as lossy, application oriented compression techniques. They generally have the net effective of maximizing the available capacity based on the goals of the service provider. These benefits vary by application but are substantial enough that virtually any data application over satellite should consider the use of PEP technology, with the one exception being live streaming video applications which typically are pre-compressed and are delivered via UDP.

PEPs can be proprietary or standards-based. The dominant standards-based solution is SCPS-TP [3], or the associated I-PEP [4] standard developed by the SatLabs Group. Modern PEPs are generally user transparent. SCPS-TP and I-PEP also are by default network transparent; they use an enhanced TCP approach that retains the IP address and port numbers during and through acceleration. The SCPS-TP approach of using an enhanced TCP (with more options) also benefits from being able to incorporate ongoing enhancements, drawn from the research community, directly to the PEP.

3 Satellite PEP Deployment Scenarios

There are many factors to be considered for the deployment of PEP technology into networks incorporating satellite-based technology as a primary communications basis. This section will review and comment on the PEP technology aspect.

3.1 Optimization of VSATs

The dominant scenario, and best understood, is of course to deploy PEP technology closely bracketing the satellite link on VSAT networks. TCP acceleration can be integrated and deployed within a terminal itself. As the TCP protocol particularly suffers on networks with variable latency and bandwidth, TCP acceleration technology has been commonly integrated for some time. Integrated TCP acceleration in the terminal unit is also becoming common on more traditional SCPC links as well. With the historical price sensitivity satellite modem manufacturers face, these modems did not make use of more advanced processors and thus often provide little benefit beyond TCP acceleration and enforcing QoS on the available bandwidth. Meanwhile, there is demonstrated benefit to compression and other techniques to optimize the bandwidth that has not been deployed significantly as of yet. However with continued increase in the CPU power and memory availability compared to the relatively modest increases in terminal bandwidths, this can be expected to change. Embedded optimization in the terminal will provide substantial benefit both to the user in terms of response time and to the operator in terms of capacity. However, the embedded PEP technique will only act on TCP/IP data that has not been encrypted so it is generally applied to Internet access and various commercial services.

PEP technology can be deployed on a stand-alone, dedicated purpose basis (as a network appliance) or incorporated with other network appliance technologies such as VPN.

Network layer encryption such as IPSec completely hides the TCP layer headers from acceleration devices, as such it cannot benefit from acceleration. Proper encryption also has the property of randomizing the data, rendering it uncompressible and inaccessible to application layer optimization. SSL based VPNs can have the SSL element accelerated, but not the encapsulated TCP/IP data so the problem persists.

Notably, IPSec would normally be preferred over SSL-based VPNs, as SSL VPNs use TCP thus doubly complicating the issues with the TCP protocol. While the actual TCP, or the SSL-TCP may be accelerated, there are actually two levels of TCP to be accelerated (TCP-in-TCP) and so the solution will still suffer from standard TCP's limitations and poor performance.

3.2 Mobile Satellite Services Optimization

Mobile Satellite Services (MSS) further adds a new set of challenges for a PEP manufacturer; including more demand on bandwidth, more susceptibility to link outages, routing flexibility for multiple communication paths (possibly both satellite and terrestrial) and the resulting adaptation required for links with dramatically different characteristics including jitter, latency, peak and minimum bandwidth and asymmetry. In addition to effectively serve the MSS market one must consider in particular physical characteristics that properly consider the deployment environment.

In the transportation sector, multiple access techniques may be made available. These are often configured independently from a PEP: a tunnel through multiple alternate network paths may be setup to isolate the remote network, yet they can lead to substantial changes in the characteristics in link. This is common of ships and aircraft which may need to employ alternate technologies or frequencies based on their location, as well as access technique. For instance, a ship may use VSAT technology at sea, switch to BGAN as they enter a country's waters and may no longer be licensed to use the VSAT technology, and change yet again to a wired or wireless as they enter a harbor.

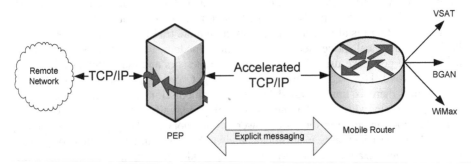

Fig. 1. Explicit messaging between elements to signal link changes

The use of a network transparent optimization protocol, where the accelerated connections carry the same IP addresses, port numbers and appropriate DSCP tags can be easier to use. The caveat for new PEP installations is to be wary of intermediate shaping devices already deployed which may attempt to shape the accelerated traffic downwards and work against the TCP acceleration.

A single-configuration "best fit" TCP acceleration scenario using a preset congestion control strategy (e.g. TCP NewReno, Vegas or Westwood or some other proprietary congestion control algorithm), while worthy of further research, currently cannot provide the effective solution for all deployment., Hence this approach lowers the delivered bandwidth and ultimately the competitiveness of a network solution incorporating satellites. However, in cases where a VPN exists between the PEP and the mobile router, a best fit solution is the only option however explicit probing or artificial intelligence techniques could be used to determine the type of link in actual use and reconfigure accordingly.

A PEP manufacturer can provide an interface to a middleware component which could be written to adapt the TCP acceleration and possibly other elements to changes in the link characteristics if they are known. Such a configuration means that an adaptive congestion control can be avoided, and a more aggressive congestion control approach can be used to maximize throughput.

There is no standard at this time for such an interface: in part this is due to the different information that may be available. The information in the message could take the form of an explicit rate, a profile referencing a specific link technology, a value representing available buffer space in bytes (possibly in a matrix referenced by different queues), the latency, bit error rate or jitter. Depending on the PEP, it could provide benefit to communicate these bandwidth properties to the other PEPs in the system. This could be done with an extended I-PEP option for instance.

This market also often demands more bandwidth that can be readily supplied by current MSS services such as Inmarsat's BGAN service. While very bandwidth scalable VSAT terminals now exist, the same can not be said of most MSS services without a dramatic increase in cost and physical deployment size. As these networks use shared contention strategies of some kind and make use of multiple hops, they can also deliver less bandwidth that expected; for instance an FTP transfer through BGAN can be expected to go between 150kbps and 300kbps *[inmarsat reference]* despite the maximum terminal capacity of 492 kbps. TCP acceleration can double the link utilization. Then other improvements further multiply the benefit: compression can improve the performance anywhere from zero for pre-compressed video, a typical 2:1 to higher compression ratios for text and raw sensor data, as well as minimize the data consumption bill for per-per-bit services. PEP technology can then be considered to help bridge modern broadband MSS services to VSAT technologies.

The deployment of such PEP technology into these MSS must be accessible and affordable. The demand for something portable has driven XipLink, Inc. to release a 'XipStick'; a network appliance smaller than a typical compact mobile phone. It provides two Ethernet interfaces, a USB which can be used for power as well as a USB-based network interface for a laptop. This makes it an ideal deployment platform for typical MSS terminals and be carried in one's pocket. The standalone nature permits government level encryption devices to be used in line, or it can also provide secure IPSec-based VPN services. Unlike PC software solutions, it can also act on all data from a network intelligently, and there is no PC software to maintain. Remarkable for this discussion is that this compactness and computing power (sufficient for intelligent compression strategies) at a reasonable price level simply was not available until recently.

Communications systems for aircraft obviously have their own challenges for the certification of equipment installed on an aircraft. The importance for PEP technology to operate on general purpose hardware is further reinforced by this market and many similar certification-heavy environments. A software embedded PEP can be used with pre-certified hardware equipment in order to shorten the time to deploy the system.

The configuration of the hub-based system tends to be different on MSS systems as well. Typical MSS only has a small number of terminals connected and transmitting at any one time. As well, they are less likely to share a receive channel and instead behave more like a dedicated link attempting to traverse a shared network, such that

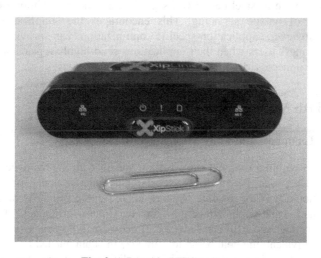

Fig. 2. A Portable PEP Appliance

they have an upper boundary on their maximum bandwidth. In the case of BGAN networks, a hub PEP system needs to treat each remote BGAN terminal as an individual basis with a fixed maximum. This is different than the VSAT scenario with many terminals sharing a DVB receive path, allowing unused bandwidth can be redistributed and shared amongst the active terminals.

3.3 PEP Client Software Based Solutions

A PC-based software solution can be an option for the deployment of PEP technology for both VSAT and MSS markets. Although this obviously eases additional hardware issues, there continues to be considerable hesitancy for service providers to put themselves in a position to be maintaining PC software and the impacts of different operating systems, service packs and other applications which may interfere. Furthermore, if there is more users on a network accessing a terminal a PC based solution will not be aware of the network utilization of the other nodes and therefore must use less effective adaptive congestion control techniques: there is benefit to a funneled solution where one node will see all of the traffic on the network. However a software-based solution has the benefit of end-to-end VPN possibilities if installed in the operating system in such a way that it is applied before the VPN tunnel is created. This approach is particularly attractive for employees who find themselves only occasionally accessing the network over satellite and a corporate IT department has mandated a particular PC-based VPN client.

The satellite-based service provider has a similar issue with IT infrastructure maintenance; most providers position themselves to provide access. The use of application-specific optimization creates a grey area; when provided by a service provider it is more likely to confuse service provision with IT services to properly maintain application-specific optimization as the application specific optimization must be updated with new versions and changes to the IT infrastructure. This is of particular importance to satellite networks given the wide distribution of nodes and the difficulties of on-site servicing. This encourages the simplification of PEP technology. However, application-specific optimization can provide substantial benefits for business users when their applications send highly repeatable data or the applications are unnecessarily highly interactive.

4 Bandwidth Management

4.1 Remote Terminals and Fully Meshed Networks

PEPs embedded within a terminal can work in tandem with the bandwidth allocation mechanisms. They can be made to substantially increase the performance of networks, particularly if the satellite network is configured primarily or entirely in a demand-assigned bandwidth allocation for maximum efficiency. Coordination between the terminal and PEP can have the effect of making congestion control and flow control equivalent: the goal being to right size the data queued to send within the terminal. This section revisits the generalized explicit messaging scenario as depicted by Figure 1, but focuses specifically on a dedicated link to be optimized.

The queue size in the output buffer of the TDMA modem should not be so much as to increase latency unnecessarily, and not so little that the terminal cannot assert to the bandwidth controller that it is demanding resource of the network. This can allow the system to minimize buffering of bulk (TCP) data. On most TDMA networks, this queue length can vary dramatically on a millisecond basis, as they typically use a burst time plan between 30ms to 120ms, so such a solution must be highly reactive.

However the coordination between the terminal and the PEP is not possible when VPN is enabled between the PEP and the satellite modem. Indeed this is a major driver of sales of standalone units to networks that already have TCP acceleration embedded in the terminals. At least in many government level encryption solutions, the VPN prevents devices within the network from communicating directly the external entity outside of the network. However intelligent algorithms best-fit have been implemented that permit 100% utilization of the TDMA link return channel. However unlike some of the mobility applications described above, this is specific to one link technology. The proper implementation of DSCP (which is promoted through the encryption process) will allow simultaneous real-time data such as VOIP to flow properly into the right queues.

4.2 Hub PEP Issues

Adaptive Coding and Modulation (ACM) adds further challenges to the hub as the effective bandwidth to any terminal may change; thus requiring flexibility to shift bandwidth allocations and in order to maintain Service Level Agreements (SLAs). The combination of ACM, QoS/shaping/SLA enforcement, TCP acceleration and advanced compression creates many challenges. Namely, they all may act at different layers of the network stack: link layer, IP layer, TCP layer respectively and the compression which may exist in some form at any layer. Thus cross-layer and likely cross-device interaction between the devices/functions can be very significant in support of developing optimal hub configuration.

For instance, if the PEP is installed downstream of the shaping device, then the traffic will be shaped prior to compression and the bandwidth possibly under-utilized. If the PEP is installed prior to the shaping device, then the PEP may be forced to run in an adaptive congestion control to allow the shaper to shape, or it must mirror the shaper configuration. Feedback systems, such as the one described earlier, can be developed, or a completely integrated solution can be deployed. QoS within the PEP system can allow it mirror the network properties and use a more aggressive bandwidth control mechanism instead of an adaptive congestion control algorithm.

System scalability is a key issue for the acceleration of Internet traffic. For public networks, it can be seen that the number of TCP connections transiting the hub can be very high, particularly in areas where PCs are poorly maintained the network is rife with viruses. Peer to peer and other applications further load the network. It has been seen that the use of Satellite for backhaul network applications may use two orders of magnitude greater TCP connections than private or government networks.

4.3 Comments

Application specific PEPs fail to yield the important benefits from a generalized technology. General PEP technology providers need to be flexible to fully address the specific needs of particular TCP/IP applications performed over different satellite-based technologies, as well as terrestrial wireless and even wired configurations. An important aspect of this is flexibility for PEP TCP acceleration, independently in each direction.

The availability of affordable but reasonably advanced processors yields new opportunities for inline streaming compression. The compelling economics of advanced optimization, while beyond the scope of this paper, must be more thoroughly considered by the satellite industry. The use of various bandwidth management techniques, compression, shared caches or data suppression techniques must also be considered in view of the network topology and scale and the PEPs must be adaptable to new requirements.

References

1. Border, J., et al.: Performance Enhancing Proxies Intended to Mitigate Link-Related Degradations, RFC 3135 (June 2001)
2. Consultative Committee for Space Data Systems, Space Communications Protocol Specification (SCPS): Transport Protocol, CCSDS-714.0-B-1,
   http://www.ccsds.org
3. The SatLabs Group, http://www.satlabs.org
4. RFC 2474 – Definition of the Differentiated Services Field (DS) in the IPv4 and IPv6 Headers

High Altitude Platforms: Radio Resource Management Policy for MBMS Applications

Alessandro Raschellà, Giuseppe Araniti, Antonio Iera, and Antonella Molinaro

ARTS Laboratory - Dept. DIMET - University "Mediterranea" of Reggio Calabria,
Reggio Calabria, Italy
{alessandro.raschella,araniti,antonio.iera,
antonella.molinaro}@unirc.it

Abstract. In this work we are interested in investigating how the High Altitude Platform (HAP) can efficiently support Multimedia Broadcast/Multicast Service (MBMS) in a scenarios wherein the terrestrial network is not available. To this aim, we propose to implement an efficient policy of Radio Resources Management (RRM) into the HAP Radio Network Controller (H-RNC). The proposed technique allows to improve the overall system capacity by selecting the most efficient multicast transport channel in terms of power consumption and by defining the switching thresholds between point-to-point and point-to-multipoint connections.

Keywords: HAP, Radio Resource Management, MBMS, Multicast transmission.

1 Introduction

The widespread diffusion of new services, such as for example video conferencing or streaming, into the cellular environment has originated the need for a point-to-multipoint (PtM) communication modality supporting information exchange among one sender and several mobile receivers. Therefore, the third generation partnership project (3GPP) introduced a new protocol, called Multimedia Broadcast/Multicast Service (MBMS), to the purpose of providing *groups oriented* services. Notwithstanding, a terrestrial-only MBMS segment may still be inadequate to environments showing high exacting communication requirements. It is the case of so called disadvantaged areas; for instance, either rural areas or areas involved in unpredictable catastrophic incidents. Advantages deriving from the MBMS extension to space-terrestrial integrated platforms, known as Satellite-MBMS (S-MBMS) [1], [2] are manifest; they are mainly related to: wider coverage area capability, reduction of terrestrial segment overloading, overall cost reduction as a consequence of multicast service delivery to more users within the same coverage area, etc. In spite of the highlighted advantages, the use of satellites implies severe limitations, mainly due to well known features, such as: heterogeneity of the channel quality, long propagation delays (in case of geostationary ,GEO, satellites) and high complexity (in case of low-Earth orbit, LEO, satellites).

K. Sithamparanathan (Ed.): Psats 2009, LNICST 15, pp. 85–93, 2009.
© ICST Institute for Computer Sciences, Social-Informatics and Telecommunications Engineering 2009

High Altitude Platforms (HAPs) are a valid space segment alternative to satellites in supporting MBMS services and applications, particularly when disadvantages areas are taken into account. HAPs are stratospheric platforms, usually located at an altitude of 17-22 km, which may be effectively regarded as a very low satellite. Some of the advantages have been clearly highlighted in [3] and can be summarized in the following: rapid deployment, broadband capability, large area coverage, very large system capacity, low propagation delay. Moreover, HAPs could be either utilized as base stations in the sky (*standalone* case) or as an overlapping coverage (*integrated system* case). In this work we consider the former case, because we are interested to investigate how the HAP can efficiently support the MBMS services in a scenario wherein the terrestrial network is not available.

To this aim, we foresee to implement in the HAP Radio Network Controller (RNC) an efficient policy of Radio Resources Management (RRM). It has to reduce as much as possible the power consumed by a HAP base station, for a given *multicast group*. The saved power will allow to increase the overall system capacity while reducing the impact of multicast services on the pre-existing unicast traffic; both traffic typologies, in fact, share the same radio resource. The limitation in the power that the transmitter can use to deliver multicast traffic, pushes towards the wise selection of the most efficient transport channel in terms of power consumption. MBMS services can utilize over the radio interface *Common* (Forward Access Channel, FACH), *Dedicated* (Dedicated Channel, DCH) and *Shared* transport channel (High Speed Downlink Shared Channel, HS-DSCH). Power saving is related to the number of users receiving MBMS data; in fact, if such number increases, then one needs a higher amount of DCHs; this reducing the resources made available to unicast traffic. It is, therefore, important to decide the maximum number of multicast users using the DCHs that allows a power saving. Such a number represents a very useful threshold to switch from dedicated channel to either common or shared ones (these being channel, which instead allow to provide multicast services utilizing a fixed amount of power, regardless of multicast users number). The sought power threshold depends on *(i)* the distance from the centre of the area covered by the HAP; *(ii)* the application bit rate.

The state of the art in term of MBMS radio resource optimization witnesses to the great amount of work that has been conducted on *Switching Thresholds* investigations only considering the UMTS terrestrial network [4], [5], [6]. The present paper contributes to the advance of the state-of-the-art in that our RRM policy gives a novel contribution to the definition of the *Switching Thresholds* from *Dedicated* to *Common* channels, when considering MBMS transmissions from HAPs systems in a standalone case.

The paper is structured as follows. Section 2 provides a brief overview of the integration of HAPs into the MBMS architecture. Section 3 describes the transport channels features considered in our research work, for multicast transmissions from the HAPs. Main results of a simulation campaign aiming at defining the RRM policy are the focus of Section 4. Conclusive remarks are given in Section 5.

2 MBMS/HAP Architecture

A possible modality for including HAPs into a MBMS architecture to provide multicast/broadcast service delivery is shown in Figure 1. It implies the addition of an

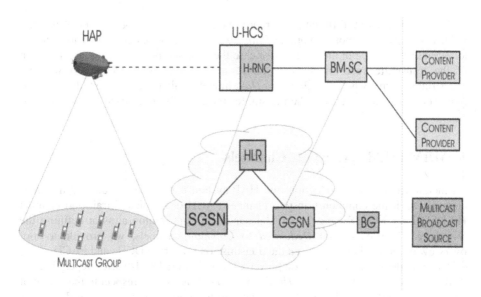

Fig. 1. MBMS/HAPs Architecture

UMTS-HAP Control System (U-HCS) to the MBMS architecture, with functionality of Radio Network Controller (H-RNC).

HAP carries a UMTS payload, at an altitude of 22 km above the service area. Therefore, Figure 1 highlights the node of the UMTS terrestrial network used in a HAP system. In particular, we can notice the presence of the following elements: *SGSN (Serving GPRS Support Node)* that carries out user individual service control functions and gathers together all individual users of the same MBMS service into a single *MBMS group*; *GGSN (Gateway GPRS Support Node)* that terminates the MBMS GTP tunnels from the SGSN and links these tunnels with the MBMS data source via IP multicast; *BM-SC (Broadcast-Multicast Service Center)* that is the new element introduced into such an architecture to provide MBMS data.

Even if the proposed MBMS/HAP architecture seems to show a behaviour very close to the MBMS/UMTS terrestrial network [7] one, notwithstanding several important differences (reported in Table 1) between *terrestrial* and *space* segments needs to be taken into account to determine the right *Switching Thresholds*.

Table 1. MBMS/UMTS terrestrial network *vs* MBMS/HAP system

Features	Terrestrial Wireless	HAP
Breadth of geographical coverage	A few kilometres per base station	Hundreds of kilometres per platform (up to 200km)
Cell diameter	0.1 – 1 km	1 – 10 km
Shadowing from terrain	Causes gaps in coverage; requires additional equipment	Problem only at low elevation angles
Antenna Gain	Constant	Variable
Path Loss	Okumura Hata	Free Space

The most evident difference is represented by the propagation environment. Indeed, HAPs enjoy more favorable *Path Loss* characteristics compared to wireless terrestrial links, since in the *Free Space* case the received power decays as a function of the transmitter-receiver distance raised to a power of 2. While, in wireless terrestrial systems, where the *Okumura Hata* model is taken into account, the received power decays as a function of the transmitter-receiver distance raised to a power of 4 [6].

3 MBMS/HAP Transport Channels

As mentioned in the introduction, the HAP system can use the dedicated transport channel DCH, the common transport channel FACH or the shared transport channel HS-DSCH for MBMS applications. As our novel contribution aims at defining the *Switching Thresholds* from *Dedicated* to *Common* channels, we provide a brief overview of the modality to assign the transmission power to DCHs and FACH.

The total downlink transmission power allocated to the DCHs varies depending on: *(i)* the number of multicast users; *(ii)* the position of users with respect to the centre of the area covered by theHAP, (for instance, users close to the centre need a lower amount of power than users at cell border); *(iii)* the application bit rate. Equation (1) defines the total transmission power assigned to a number of DCHs equal to "i" scattered in a given cell [8].

$$P_{T,i} = (C/I)_i \frac{\sum_{j=1}^{N_c} G(\theta_j,d_j)P_T + (1-\alpha)P_{Tot(i-1)}G(\theta_i,d_i) + P_p G(\theta_i,d_i) + N_d}{G(\theta_i,d_i)} \qquad (1)$$

Where N_c is the number of interfering neighboring cells, P_T is the interference from such cells, α is the orthogonality factor that can be zero in the case of perfect orthogonality, $P_{Tot(i-1)}$ is the power allocated to a number of users equal to *i-1*, P_p is the power devoted to common control channels, N_d is the Additive Gaussian White Noise (AGWN). While $G(\theta_j, d_j)$ is the link gain and *C/I* is the Carrier-to-Interference ratio, calculated by Equation 2 and 3 respectively.

$$G(\theta_i,d_i)_{dB} = g(\theta_i)_{dB} - L_p(d_i)_{dB} \qquad (2)$$

$$(C/I)_{dB} = (E_b/N_0)_{dB} - (G_p)_{dB} \qquad (3)$$

Where θ_i is the angle representing the boresight direction [9], $g(\theta_i)$ is the *Antenna Gain* calculated in the boresight direction, $L_p(d_i)$ is the attenuation value caused by the *Path Loss* for the user at a distance equal to d_i from the centre of the area covered by the HAP. While E_b/N_0 is the Energy per Bit-to-Spectral Noise Density and G_p is the Processing Gain.

A FACH channel transmits at a fixed power level, since fast power control is not supported in this kind of channel. It is a PtM channel and must be received by all UEs throughout the cell covered by the HAP, regardless of the considered *Path Loss* and

Antenna Gain. Therefore, the fixed power has to be high enough to guarantee the services in the whole coverage area [10]. The bit rate of the MBMS services and the needed coverage area of the cell affect the allocated power for the FACH channel. The delivery of high data rate MBMS services over FACH is not always feasible, since excessive downlink transmission power would be required. High bit rates can only be offered to users located very close to the centre of the area covered by the HAP.

4 Obtained Results

An exhaustive simulation campaign has been conducted to define a RRM policy aimed to select the advisable *Switching Thresholds* from *Dedicated* to *Common* channels, considering MBMS transmissions from HAPs systems in a *standalone* case. Table 2 summarizes the main considered assumptions [11], [12]. Parameters not listed are varying during the different campaigns.

Table 2. Simulation Campaign Assumptions

Parameter	Value
HAP High	22 Km
Cell Radius	2.6 Km
Cell Layout	Hexagonal grid
Number of Neighboring Cells	7
Maximum BS Tx Power	40 W
Other BS Tx Power	10 W
Common Channel Power	2 W
Path Loss	Free Space
Multipath Channel	Vehicular A (3Km/h)
Orthogonality Factor	0,5
BLER Target	1 %
Gmax	32,3 dBi
Thermal Noise	-100 dBm
Application Bit Rate	64, 128, 256 Kbps

In Figure 2 the *Switching Thresholds* are defined when 64 kbps is the considered bit rate. Moreover, to highlight how the user mobility and position can affect the proposed RRM algorithm, three situations have been investigated in which multicast users are scattered respectively within 50%, 75% and 95% of cell coverage size. From Figure 2, it clearly emerges that the DCHs behavior weakly depends on the users position, while the FACH assigned power strictly depend on the covered area and, hence, on the position of the farter multicast user (5.6 W, 8.8 W and 15.2 W for 50%, 75% and 95% of cell coverage size respectively).

The difference between DCHs and FACH behavior is due to a different modality in assigning the channel transmission power, as explained in Section 3. Hence, for 64 kbps, in the worst situation, the maximum power needed to provide MBMS services in the area is equal to 15,2 W. The remaining 24,8 W could be used to serve unicast applications.

According to our RRM policy, the HAP RNC continuously keeps track of both position and number of multicast users that utilize DCH channels. In so doing, the RNC can decide the power to assign to the FACH and, as a consequence, the *Switching Thresholds*. In particular, when multicast users are scattered within 50%, 75% and 95% of area covered by the HAP, the *Switching Thresholds* from DCHs to FACH are equal to 34, 44 and 55 respectively.

Similar considerations can be made for 128 and 256 kbps applications, illustrated in Figure 3 and 4 respectively. As shown in the figures, FACH channel requires a higher power with respect to the previous case. In particular, when 128 kbps is the application bit rate, an amount of power equal to 31,6 W is needed when 95% is the cell coverage.

For this reasons, for 128 kbps, our proposed RRM policy allows to utilize FACH channel up to 75% of cell coverage and the remaining multicast users will be served by DCH channels. This choice enables to save a sufficient amount of power (about 50%) for unicast users and allows to obtain interesting results in term of Grade of Services for both unicast and multicast traffic. Hence, when multicast users are scattered within 50% and 75% of area covered by the HAP and 128 kbps is the service bit rate, then the *Switching Thresholds* from DCHs to FACH are equal to 28 and 32 users respectively.

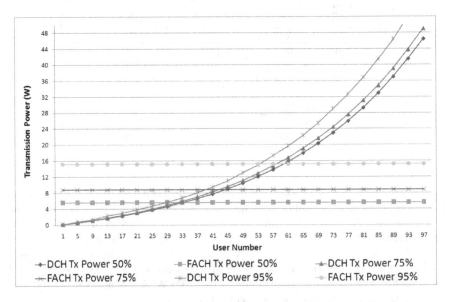

Fig. 2. Tx power vs. Cell Coverage for applications with a bit rate of 64 kbps

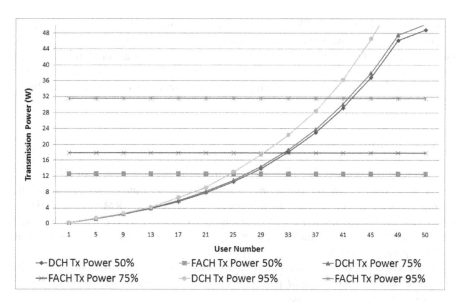

Fig. 3. Tx power vs. Cell Coverage for applications with a bit rate of 128 kbps

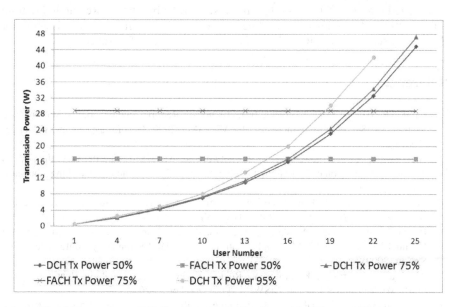

Fig. 4. Tx power vs. Cell Coverage for applications with a bit rate of 256 kbps

In case of 256 kbps services the FACH transmission power is not defined for a cell coverage equal to 95%, because the required power would be greater than the overall HAP transmission power. Hence, when the application bit rate is equal to 256 kbps, the *Switching Thresholds* are defined only for 50% and 75% cell coverage and are equal to 16 and 20 users respectively.

Moreover, when the FACH is active to cover a given area, some of the served MBMS user could leave the *multicast group*. In this case, the RRM policy allows the system to check if the exploitation of DCH channels becomes again more efficient, in term of power consumption, than the use of FACH. Therefore, the switching from FACH to DCHs channels is performed, this leaving further resource available to unicast traffic.

5 Conclusion

In providing MBMS services the choice of the most efficient transport channel is a key aspect, since a wrong transport channel selection could adversely affect the overall capacity of the system. In this paper we defined a RRM policy aiming at identifying the best *Switching Thresholds* among DCH and FACH channels, by taking into account the radio channel conditions, the cell coverage radius, and two sample MBMS application bit rates.

Obtained results demonstrate that a smart selection of transport channels coupled to the use of the proposed *RRM* policy, leads to an efficient management of MBMS services in a HAP standalone scenario.

Acknowledgments. This work has been supported by Italian Research Program (PRIN 2007) Satellite-Assisted Localization and Communication system for Emergency services (SALICE). Web site: http://lenst.det.unifi.it/salice

References

1. ETSI TR 101 865 V1.2.1 (2002-09), Technical Report, Satellite Earth Stations and Systems (SES); Satellite component of UMTS/IMT-2000; General aspects and principles (2002)
2. Narenthiran, K., et al.: S-UMTS access network for MBMS service delivery: the SATIN approach. International Journal of Satellite Communications and Networking (January-February 2004)
3. Tozer, T.C., Grace, D.: Broadband Service Delivery from High Altitude Platforms, Sector: Next Generation Networks. In: COMMUNICATE (2000)
4. Raschellà, A., Umbert, A., Araniti, G., Iera, A., Molinaro, A.: SINR-based Transport Channel Selection for MBMS Application. In: Vehicular Techonology Conference: VTC-Spring (2009)
5. Alexiou, A., Bouras, C., Kokkinos, V., Rekkas, E.: Power Efficient Radio Bearer Selection in MBMS Multicast Mode. In: MSWIM 2007, October 22-26 (2007)
6. IST-2001-35125 (OverDRiVE), Deliverable of the project (D08): Spectrum Efficient Multicast and Asymmetric Services in UMTS
7. Karapantazis, S., Pavlidou Aristotle, F.-N.: Broadband Communications via High Altitude Platforms (HAPs) – A survey. IEEE Communications Letters (2005)
8. Taha-Ahmed, B., Calvo-Ramòn, M., de Haro-Ariet, L.: On the High Altitude Platfom (HAP) W-CDMA System Capacity. Radio engineering 13(2) (2004)

9. Thornton, J., Grace, D., Capstick, M.H., Tozer, T.C.: Optimizing an Array of Antennas for Cellular Coverage From a High Altitude Platform. IEEE Transactions on Wireless Communications (2003)
10. IST-2003-507607 (B-BONE). Deliverable D2.5. Final results with combined enhancements of the air interface
11. Falletti, E., Mondin, M., Dovis, F., Grace, D.: Integration of a HAP within a Terrestrial UMTS Network, Wireless Personal Communications, Netherlands (2003)
12. Grace, D., Spillard, C., Thornton, J., Tozer, T.C.: Channel assignment strategies for a high altitude platform spot-beam architecture. In: IEEE PIMRC (2002)

Frequency Tracking Performance Using a Hyperbolic Digital-Phase Locked Loop for Ka-Band Communication in Rain Fading Channels

Kandeepan Sithamparanathan and Radoslaw Piesiewicz

Create-Net International Research Centre,
via alla Cascata 56/D, Trento, 38100, Italy
{Kandee,Radoslaw.Piesiewicz}@create-net.org

Abstract. In this paper we study and present some results on the performances of frequency tracking for Ka-band satellite communications in rain fading channels. The carrier frequency is tracked using a 2nd order hyperbolic phase detector based digital-phase locked loop (D-PLL). The hyperbolic D-PLL has the capability of extending the tracking range compared to the other D-PLL and hence can be designed such that to achieve low phase jitter performance for improved carrier tracking. We present the design and analysis of the D-PLL and show some simulation results on the frequency tracking performance for Ka-band rain fading channel. The results are compared with the non-fading noise only case and comparative analyses are made.

Keywords: Frequency tracking, digital-phase locked loops, hyperbolic phase detector, Ka-band frequency tracking.

1 Introduction

Higher frequency transmission for satellite communication is of great interest in the current era to have high speed video transmission and broadband internet access. The currently available Ka-frequency-band, with 30GHz uplink and 20GHz downlink for satellite communications, is one of the frequency bands that could deliver such high speed communication links to and from the satellites by exploiting the wider bandwidth available at such frequencies.

Frequency synchronization is quite crucial for high speed communication especially at higher frequencies such as for the Ka-band. Excess frequency or phase jitter in the receiver may lead up to losing the link, especially when the received signal power is quite low, due to increasing bit errors cause due to synchronization errors. Hence precise frequency synchronization is considered to be very crucial especially at higher frequency bands. In general, a standard level of jitter can be accepted in order to achieve a certain value of probability of bite error at the receiver, however when there is fading, the signal level fluctuation (signal power fluctuation) may lead to excess jitter in the estimated frequency leading towards unacceptable levels of bit error rates. In this paper we study the performance of frequency tracking using digital-phase locked loop (D-PLL) under rain fading conditions for the Ka-band

K. Sithamparanathan (Ed.): Psats 2009, LNICST 15, pp. 94–102, 2009.

channel. There exist several feed forward and feedback frequency synchronization techniques [10] however D-PLL is considered to be computationally efficient which draws our interest.

Digital-phase locked loops are used to track signal frequencies in communication systems [3,5] for local frequency synchronization. Traditionally the phase locked loops have a trade-off between the acquisition performance and the tracking performance based on the loop parameter known as the closed loop bandwidth B_L. Having a higher value for the loop bandwidth enables to acquire wider range of frequencies but at the same time increases the phase noise during tracking after acquiring the frequency. The increase in phase noise (hence the increase in the instantaneous frequency jitter) will degrade the probability of bit error at the receiver. The hyperbolic phase detector based digital phase locked loop [4] due to its nonlinear characteristics enhances the tracking range of the frequency, which then allows us to reduce the value of B_L (note that B_L is defined only with respect to a linear loop [3,5]) for the corresponding phase locked loop and hence reducing the phase jitter during the tracking mode compared to the standard digital phase locked loop.

In this paper we study the performance of such a hyperbolic digital phase locked loop when it is used to track carrier frequencies for Ka-band satellite communications under rainy fading channel conditions. The Hyperbolic D-PLL is used due to its extended tracking capabilities instead of the standard D-PLL [4]. We consider the baseband system model in our analysis and track the frequency error present at the baseband signal. In [4] the loop model for the hyperbolic digital phase locked loop is presented and the performance analysis of the loop is also studied for the additive Gaussian noise only case. In this paper we consider a similar model for the phase locked loop and extend the analysis for a Ka-band fading channel with additive noise.

The rest of the paper is composed with the following sections. In Section-2 and Section-3 we provide the communications system model at Ka-band and the loop model for the hyperbolic digital phase locked loop, respectively. In Section-4 we present some theoretical analysis on the phase locked loop for non-fading conditions, and in Section-5 we present some simulation results on the performance of the phase locked loop and compare the results with the non-fading theoretical case. Finally, we provide some concluding remarks.

2 Communication System and Ka-Band Channel Models

Figure-1 shows the communication system model that is considered in our work. At the transmitter on the satellite, the raw digital data is mapped into symbols and passed trough the pulse shaping filter to band limit the signal to reduce inter symbol interference. The pulse shaping filter used here is the square root raised cosine filter with a roll factor α defining the bandwidth of the transmitted signal. The filtered signal is then passed through a QPSK modulator before transmitting it through a parabolic dish antenna thorough the Ka-band communication channel. The Ka-band communication channel is modeled as a rainy fading channel as described in [6]. The received signal is then demodulated and processed for signal frequency, timing and phase synchronization in order to detect and decode the received symbols.

In our model we assume perfect timing synchronization in order to make the analysis easier, and furthermore we do not consider any channel equalizer specifically to analyze the performance of frequency tracking under rain fading conditions. The received baseband signal in its complex envelope form is given by,

$$r = h(t)s(t) + n(t) \tag{1}$$

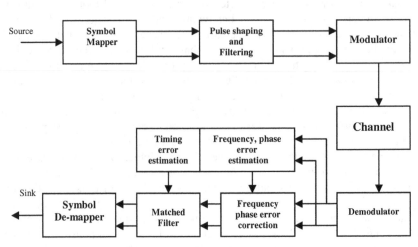

Fig. 1. The Communication System model considered to analyse the performance of the Hyperbolic Digital- Phase Locked Loop

where, $h(t)$ is the rain fading channel at Ka-band in its complex envelope form given by,

$$h(t) = h\_I(t)+jh\_Q(t) \tag{2}$$

where h_I and h_Q follow the statistical distribution as described in [6]. We follow the method described in [6] to model the rain fading channel, and the readers are recommended to read [6] for a detailed explanation of the channel model. The complex envelope $s(t)$ of the received signal at the baseband, with a bandwidth of Bw and a frequency error of Δf which is to be tracked, is given by,

$$s(t) = \sum c\_m*g(t - mT)\exp(-j2\pi\Delta ft+j\beta) \tag{3}$$

where, c_m is the mth data symbol given by, $c\_m = a\_m + jb\_m$, with a_m and b_m are elements of the set $\{-1,1\}$, $g(t)$ is the square root raised cosine pulse, and T is the symbol duration. The additive noise $n(t)$ is a zero mean band limited complex Gaussian process given by,

$$n(t) = n\_I(t) + jn\_Q(t) \tag{4}$$

where, $n\_I(t)$ and $n\_Q(t)$ are the inphase and the quadrature components each with noise power of σ^2 each.

3 The Hyperbolic Digital Phase Locked Loop

The loop model considered is given in Figure-1. It consists of an error detector or a phase detector (PD), a loop filter and a numerically controlled oscillator (NCO). The NCO is equivalent to the voltage controlled oscillator (VCO) of its analog counterpart.

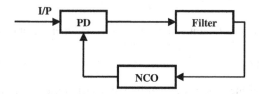

Fig. 2. Digital phase locked loop model

The PD is a four-quadrant arctan PD that maps the input arguments to its corresponding four quadrant phase plane, which is followed by a hyperbolic function. The block diagram of the PD model is shown in Figure-3. The output signal **x** from the NCO is given by,

$$x[n] = \exp\{-j\,\theta[n]\} \tag{5}$$

The multiplier in Figure-3 is a complex multiplier. The output of the multiplier is fed into the arctan function, and the resulting phase is passed through a hyperbolic function $g(.)$,

$$\varphi_e = g(\varepsilon) = \sinh(\varepsilon) \tag{6}$$

where, in (6), ε is given by,

$$\varepsilon = \arctan\{u,v\} \tag{7}$$

where, u and v are the real and imaginary components of the output of the complex multiplier as shown in Figure-3.

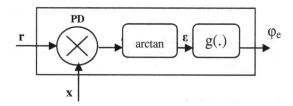

Fig. 3. The Hyperbolic phase detector model

The mathematical model of the loop without the nonlinear hyperbolic $g(.)$ function is given by its closed loop transfer function $H(z)$,

$$H(z) = \frac{D(z)V(z)}{1 + D(z)V(z)} \tag{8}$$

where, $D(z)$ and $V(z)$ are the discrete transfer functions of the loop filter and the NCO respectively, which are given by,

$$D(z) = \frac{az}{[z - (1 - a)]} \quad \text{and} \quad V(z) = \frac{k}{z - 1} \tag{9}$$

where, a is the filter co-efficient and k is the NCO parameter that controls the loop.

3.1 Lock-In Range

The lock in range of the loop is defined by the maximum frequency deviation Δf that can be locked-in by the loop. From [4] we see that the lock-in range for the D-PLL is given kf_s/2, and for the hyperbolic loop it is given by $\sinh(\pi)kf\_s/(2\pi)$, where f_s is the sampling frequency of the discrete system. From these two equations we clearly see that the hyperbolic loop can lock-in wider range of frequencies.

4 Theoretical Loop Analysis

We arte interested in the phase noise distribution of the loop for the hyperbolic phase detector based digital phase locked loop. For the additive noise only case the open loop phase noise distribution is given by,

$$f_{\varphi_e}(\varphi_e) = \cosh(\varphi_e) P_\lambda(\lambda) \tag{10}$$

where, $\lambda = \sinh^{-1}(\varphi_e)$ and $P_\lambda(\lambda)$ is given by,

$$P_\lambda(\lambda) = \begin{cases} \exp(-\rho/2)\left[\dfrac{1}{2\pi} - \exp(\dfrac{\Gamma_1}{2})(\dfrac{\Gamma_1}{2\pi})^{1/2}Q(\sqrt{\Gamma_1})\right] & \text{for } \pi/2 < \lambda \le \pi \\[4mm] \exp(-\rho/2)\left[\dfrac{1}{2\pi} + \exp(\dfrac{\Gamma}{2})(\dfrac{\Gamma}{2\pi})^{1/2}(1 - Q(\sqrt{\Gamma}))\right] & \text{for } -\pi/2 \le \lambda \le \pi/2 \\[4mm] \exp(-\rho/2)\left[\dfrac{1}{2\pi} - \exp(\dfrac{\Gamma_2}{2})(\dfrac{\Gamma_2}{2\pi})^{1/2}Q(\sqrt{\Gamma_2})\right] & \text{for } -\pi < \lambda \le -\pi/2 \end{cases} \tag{11}$$

where, ρ is the signal to noise ratio and,

$$\Gamma = \frac{\rho}{1+\alpha^2}, \ \Gamma_1 = \frac{[\tan(\pi + \alpha)\mu_1 + \mu_2]^2}{\sigma^2[1 + \tan^2(\pi + \alpha)]}, \ \Gamma_2 = \frac{[\tan(-\pi + \alpha)\mu_1 + \mu_2]^2}{\sigma^2[1 + \tan^2(-\pi + \alpha)]} \tag{12}$$

and,

$$Q(x) = \frac{1}{\sqrt{2\pi}} \int_x^\infty \exp(-u^2/2).du \ , \ \mu_1 = \sin(\varphi_{ss}), \ \mu_2 = \cos(\varphi_{ss}) \quad (13)$$

where, φ_{ss} is the steady state value of the phase error process φ_e.

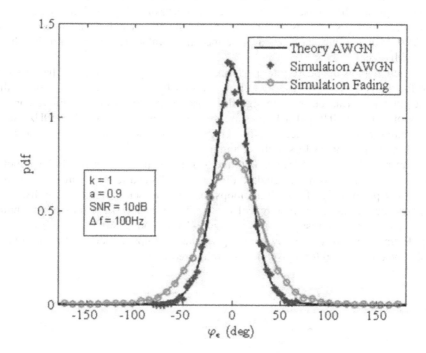

Fig. 4. the open loop phase noise distribution comparison for the hyperbolic digital phase locked loop, for AWGN noise only case and with the rain fading case

In our study we compare the statistical distribution of the phase noise in the loop for the additive noise only case and when the loop is operating in the rain fading channel environment.

The comparison study will show the differences between the two and the corresponding performance degradation under rainy fading conditions. Figure 4 depicts the phase noise distributions for the theoretical (AWGN only), simulation with AWGN only, and the simulation with rain fading environment. From the figure we clearly observe the degradation in the performance of the carrier tracking loop for the fading case, as expected. Furthermore, characterizing the noise distribution under fading conditions is also of high interest to us in order to predict the performance degradation associated with the fading conditions.

5 Phase Noise Analysis

The phase jitter analysis for the Ka-band rain fading channel is also of great interest to us in order to estimate the average bit error rate measure due to synchronization errors. Figure-5 depicts the instantaneous phase error with time for the AWGN noise only case and the rain fading case. In the figure we see some several instantaneous jumps (impulsive like noise) in the phase error process for the rain fading case due to strong/deep fading situations in the channel. On the other hand, we also observe that the AWGM noise only case has a prescribed jitter value associated with the phase error with time.

Figure-6 depicts the phase jitter performance of the hyperbolic digital phase locked loop for the AWGN only case as well as the rain fading case. The deviation in the phase jitter performance is quite significant as we observe from the figure for the values of k=0.4, a=0.9 and a frequency error at the baseband of Δf = 50Hz. Such degradation may lead to excessive bit error rate degradation and eventually leading towards an instantaneous loss of the communication link.

We also study the performance improvement in the phase jitter for the hyperbolic loop and compare it with the standard digital phase locked loop. Figure-7 shows the phase jitter performance for both the loops for a given lock in range of 2500Hz. For the given lock-in range, we require k=1 for the D-PLL and k=0.275 for the hyperbolic loop. However for the results shown in Figure-7 we choose k=0.5 for the hyperbolic loop. From the figure we clearly see the performance improvement in the phase jitter for the hyperbolic loop for a given lock-in range requirement.

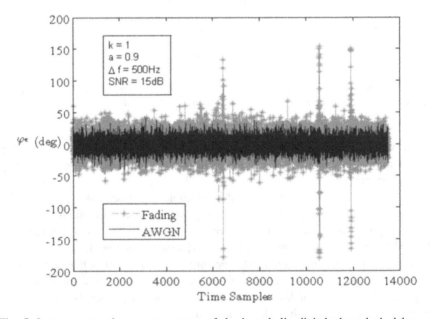

Fig. 5. Instantaneous phase error process of the hyperbolic digital phase locked loop, for AWGN only case and together with the rain fading case

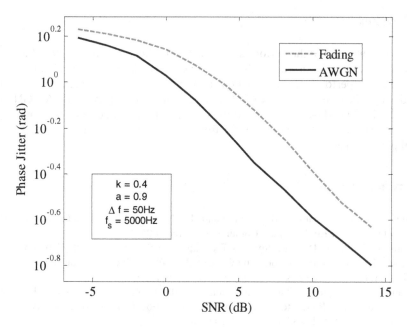

Fig. 6. Phase Jitter performance of the hyperbolic digital phase locked loop for the AWGN only case and the rain fading case

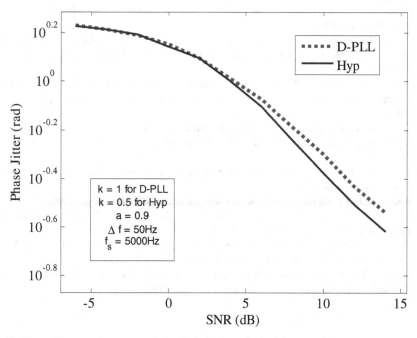

Fig. 7. Phase Jitter performance of the digital phase locked loop and the hyperbolic digital phase locked loop for the rain fading case: For a given pull-in range of 2500Hz

6 Conclusion

In this paper we studied the performance of a hyperbolic digital phase locked loop for frequency tracking for a Ka-band rain fading channel. In general conditions we observe severe performance degradation in the phase jitter performance of the phase locked loop when operating in a rain fading condition as oppose to an AWGN only channel. The hyperbolic loop, by utilizing its extended tracking (lock-in range) capability, can attain low phase jitter for frequency tracking compared to the standard digital phase locked loop.

References

1. Sun, J., Gao, J., Shambayati, S., Modiano, E.: Ka-Band Link Optimization with Rate Adaptation. In: IEEE Aerospace Conference (March 2006)
2. Satorius, E., Pinck, D.: Data Analysis Techniques for the ACTS Mobile Experiments, Jet Propulsion Laboratory, California InsWMe of Technology, Pasadena, California
3. Gardner, F.M.: Phase Lock Techniques. Willey, NY (1979)
4. Kandeepan, S.: Steady State Distribution of a Hyperbolic Digital TanLock Loop with Extended Pull-in Range for Frequency Synchronization in High Doppler Environment. IEEE Trans. of Wireless Communications (to appear)
5. Lindsey, W.C., Chie, C.M.: A Survey of DPLL. Proceedings of the IEEE, 296–317 (April 1981)
6. Fiebig, U.C.: A Time-Series Generator Modelling Rain Fading. In: Proc. Open Symposium on Propagation and Remote Sensing, URSI Commission F, Garmisch-Partenkirchen (2002)
7. Fiebig, U.C.: A Rain Fading Channel Model for Satellite Communications Links. In: Proc. Millennium Conference on Antennas and Propagation, AP 2000, Davos, Switzerland, p. 176 (2000)
8. Fiebig, U.C.: Modeling Rain Fading in Satellite Communication Links. In: Proc. Vehicular Technology Conference, VTC 1999 - Fall, Amsterdam, The Netherlands, pp. 1422–1426 (1999)
9. Kostulski, T., Reisenfeld, S.: Ka band Propagation Experiments on the Australian Low-Earth Orbit Microsatellite "FedSat". In: Australian Communications Theory Workshop 2007
10. Meyer, H., Ascheid, G.: Synchronisation in Digital Communications, vol. 1. John Willey & Sons, New York (1990)
11. Viterbi, A.J.: Principles of Coherent Comms. McGraw-Hill, New York (1966)
12. Fitz, M.P., Lindsey, W.C.: Decision-Directed Burst-Mode Carrier Synchronisation Techniques. IEEE Trans. on Comms. 40(10), 1644–1653 (1992)
13. Fitz, M.P., Cramer, R.J.-M.: A Performance Analysis of a Digital PLL Based MPSK Demodulator. IEEE Trans. on Comms. 43(2/3/4), 1192–1201 (1995)
14. Lorenzo-Ginori, J.V., Naranjo-Bouzas, J.A.: All-Digital PLL with Extended Tracking Capabilities. Electronics Letters 33(18), 1519–1521 (1997)

Design and Implementation of P2P Streaming Systems for Webcast

Yusuke Gotoh[1], Kentaro Suzuki[2], Tomoki Yoshihisa[3],
and Masanori Kanazawa[4]

[1] Graduate School of Natural Science and Technology, Okayama University,
Okayama, Japan
gotoh@cs.okayama-u.ac.jp
[2] BUFFALO INC., Nagoya, Japan
ke-suzuki@melcoinc.co.jp
[3] Cybermedia Center, Osaka University, Osaka, Japan
yoshihisa@cmc.osaka-u.ac.jp
[4] The Kyoto College of Graduate Studies for Informatics, Kyoto, Japan
bwv147@jsbach.mbox.media.kyoto-u.ac.jp

Abstract. Due to the recent spread of different styles of watching movies, streaming using Peer-to-Peer (P2P) technology has attracted great attention. In P2P streaming systems, to distribute the network load, since peers from which the user receives data are selected at random, clients have to wait until their desired data are delivered. Therefore, many researches are attempting to reduce the waiting time. However, due to the complexity of implementation, they usually evaluate these methods using machine simulations. In actual environments, interruption time is not always reduced by increasing the number of clients who deliver data. To evaluate the availability of P2P streaming systems, implementing a P2P streaming system is crucial. In this paper, we design and implement a P2P streaming system. With our implemented system, we consider situations in which the proposed system is effective.

Keywords: Broadcasting, Waiting time, Streaming, Peer-to-peer.

1 Introduction

Recently, delivery services using Internet Protocol (IP) networks have attracted much attention and are changing how we watch movies. In these services, clients connect and receive data. In on-demand type, each client demands data from a server, who replies to the demand and delivers the demanded data. Although clients can get their desired data immediately, the server's load becomes higher as the number of clients increases. When necessary bandwidth surpasses available bandwidth, the server cannot deliver data to new clients, so the waiting time from starting to receive them to starting to play them increases.

In this paper, we consider streaming delivery using P2P networks. In P2P networks, there are several clients called peers, who demand data and receive

K. Sithamparanathan (Ed.): Psats 2009, LNICST 15, pp. 103–110, 2009.

them from other peers. When a peer finishes receiving all the data, it can deliver them to other peers.

We previously proposed several scheduling methods to reduce waiting time for selecting peers on P2P streaming systems. These researches often assume a simulation environment in which load balance for receiving and playing data does not occur. However, due to the complexity of implementation, they usually evaluate these methods using machine simulation. In actual environments, waiting time is not always reduced by increasing the number of peers. To evaluate the availability of P2P streaming systems, implementing a P2P streaming system is important.

In this paper, by designing and implementing P2P streaming systems, we consider situations in which our proposed system is effective. Since it can introduce conventional scheduling methods, we can construct a delivery system based on the type of clients.

The remainder of the paper is organized as follows. Related works are explained in Section 2. Our assumed P2P streaming systems are explained in Section 3. Design and implementation are explained in Sections 4 and 5. The system is evaluated in Section 6, and discussed in Section 7. Finally, we conclude our paper in Section 8.

2   Related Works

Several P2P delivering methods have already been proposed [1, 2, 3]. In BitTorrent [4], clients receive from peers the divided data of each segment called a piece. By providing a piece of data to other peers, clients can receive other data from them. Provider peers whose available bandwidth is small can also deliver data. Since many provider peers deliver popular content, many peers can receive it on P2P networks.

Several P2P streaming methods have also been proposed [5, 6, 7]. Shah et al. proposed a scheduling method to reduce waiting time [8], in which clients receive the divided data of each segment called a piece from peers using BitTorrent. We previously proposed a scheduling method to reduce waiting time in P2P streaming called the "Waiting time Reduction for P2P Streaming (WRPS)" method [9]. In this method, waiting time is effectively reduced by sequentially receiving the first segment of data from a peer with large bandwidth. However, WRPS does not suppose the case where a provider peer concurrently delivers data to many request peers. Since the number of channels is reduced whose available bandwidth is the same as the consumption rate, waiting time increases.

3   P2P Streaming

In this section, we explain P2P streaming systems.

3.1   Peer Configuration

Our assumed P2P network structure is shown in Figure 1. In P2P networks, there are two types of peers: request and provider. In Figure 1, the request peer

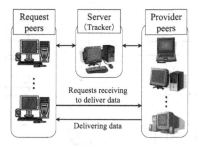

Fig. 1. Network structure in P2P streaming

is set in the center of the network and is connected to many provider peers. It demands data and receives them from provider peers using the P2P network. The request peer finishes receiving the initial part of the data and plays it. When the request peer finishes receiving all the data, it becomes the provider peer. When the request peer wants data from the provider peers, it receives data separated into segments.

When the request peer receives a segment from provider peers, waiting time occurs, so users often feel annoyed. Therefore, in P2P streaming, we need to reduce the waiting time that occurs when receiving data.

3.2 Mechanism for Waiting Time Generation

In this subsection, we explain the mechanism for waiting time generation. In conventional methods, since the request peer chooses provider peers randomly to receive some parts of the data, waiting time increases based on the selected provider peers. For example, when the request peer wants data from the provider peers and receives segment S_{i+5j} ($j = 0, \cdots, 19$) by channel b_i ($i = 1, \cdots, 5$), the delivery schedule is shown in Figure 2. The request peer is R_1, and the available bandwidth is 5.5 Mbps. Provider peers are $P_1, \cdots, P_5$. The bandwidth of b_1 is 2.0 Mbps, b_2 is 1.4 Mbps, b_3 is 0.9 Mbps, b_4 is 0.6 Mbps, and b_5 is 0.4 Mbps. The data consumption rate is 5.0 Mbps. When the data are separated into n segments, the separated segments are $S_1, \cdots, S_n$. When the total data size is 256 MB and the data size of each segment is 25.6 MB, $n = 256/25.6 = 10$. In Figure 2, when the provider peer receives S_1 for b_1, the waiting time is only the time to receive S_1, which is $256 \times 8/(2.0 \times 1000) = 1.0$ sec.

In P2P streaming, users may become annoyed when an interruption occurs between the finishing time of a segment and the starting time of the next segment. In Figure 2, when the request peer receives 22 segments, S_3, S_4, S_{5j} ($j = 1, \cdots, 20$), it plays them with interruption. In this case, the total waiting time is 59.4 sec.

In P2P streaming, clients must be able to play the data without interruptions until the end. In conventional methods, waiting time is reduced based on the available bandwidth of each provider peer. For example, in the WRPS method [9], suppose the case where the request peer delivers data that are

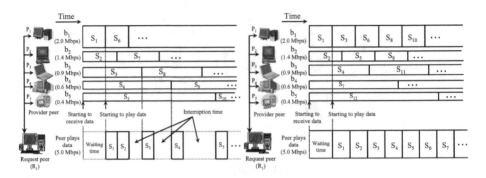

Fig. 2. Example of delivery schedule under simple method

Fig. 3. Example of delivery schedule under WRPS method

separated from 100 segments. The delivery schedule is shown in Figure 3. The WRPS method reduces waiting time by sequentially receiving the first bit of data from a peer with large bandwidth. In Figure 3, when the provider peer receives S_1 for b_1, the waiting time is only the receiving time of S_1, which is $256 \times 8/(2.0 \times 1000) = 1.0$.

3.3 Definition of Simulation Environment

Our assumed simulation environment is summarized below:

- The process time for receiving data and playing them is zero.
- In the simulation environment, we evaluate the waiting time and the interruption time by the computation simulation.
- Waiting time is calculated by computation expression.

In the simulation environment, we do not consider the process time for receiving data and playing them. In most P2P streaming methods, dividing the data into more segments further reduces waiting time.

4 Design

In this research, we design a P2P streaming system called the "Content Delivery System for P2P Streaming (DeSPerS)". Its design details are given below.

4.1 Assumed Environment

Our assumed system environment is summarized below:

- The request peer receives data from one or more provider peers.
- Provider peers have all data segments.
- Bandwidth is stable while delivering data.

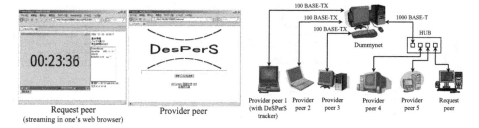

Fig. 4. Screenshot for DeSPerS

Fig. 5. Experiment environment for DeS-PerS

4.2   System Configuration

In this subsection, we explain the details of the processes in DeSPerS. As shown in Figure 1, a DeSPerS tracker plays the role of the server and manages the lists of contents and peers in the P2P networks. The list of contents is composed of a file name, a title, an abstract, a search tag, data size, and a list of the peers with appropriate data. The list of peers is composed of an IP address, a port number, and the available bandwidth of each peer.

DeSPerS uses P2P streaming in actual environments, where the following must be considered: the interruption in playing data, the load balance in delivering segments, and the overhead in receiving the data.

Interruption in playing data
In streaming delivery, since request peers can play data after receiving a given amount of buffer size, we can reduce the waiting time compared to the download type. In DeSPerS, the buffer size of the playing time of the data is 10 sec.

Load balance in delivering segment data
In P2P streaming, the size of each segment of data is set based on the software. The data size in DeSPerS is 128 KBytes. When a provider peer delivers a large amount of data at once, the delivery time using its available bandwidth becomes long. In DeSPerS, the data size is shortened by delivering the data in segments.

Overhead for receiving the data
In DeSPerS, each peer is connected by TCP / IP. For delivering data, since the provider peer appends a header to the data packet, the data size increases, and delivering time becomes longer.

5   Implementation

We implemented a P2P streaming system based on the system design. A screenshot is shown in Figure 4. In our implementation, we use a WRPS method that can easily construct a delivery schedule.

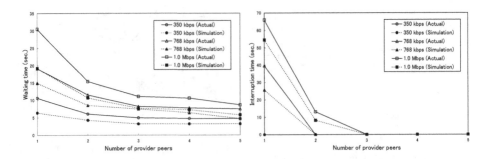

Fig. 6. Number of provider peers and average waiting time

Fig. 7. Number of provider peers and interruption time

The system configuration of DeSPerS is shown in Figure 5. To control the available bandwidth of each provider peer, we used an artificial bandwidth control machine called FreeBSD Dummynet [10]. By setting the Dummynet between the request and provider peers, the DeSPerS tracker can control the available bandwidth of each provider peer based on the network configuration.

Depending on the P2P streaming system, network configuration in actual environments can have many patterns. However, evaluating the performance of our proposed system for all of these patterns is not realistic. Therefore, we used a network configuration in which the DeSPerS tracker controls the available bandwidth of each provider peer using a Dummynet. In this system, we used six machines: one request peer, and five provider peers.

6   Evaluation

In this section, we evaluate the P2P streaming system.

6.1   Evaluation Environment

In our evaluation, the available bandwidth of each provider peer is 480, 400, 320, 240, and 160 kbps. We used the following data consumption rates: 350 kbps, 768 kbps, and 1.0 Mbps. The playing time of the data was 60 sec., and the data size of each segment was 128 Kbytes. The request peer can play the data after it finishes receiving the initial part, which is 10 sec. When there is no more data in the buffer, the request peer stops playing them and waits until it finishes receiving the data, which takes 10 sec. The data size of each segment is 128 KBytes.

6.2   Waiting Time

We calculated the average waiting time under different numbers of provider peers. The result is shown in Figure 6. The horizontal axis is the number of provider peers to which the request peer can connect. The vertical axis is the waiting time. To compare the simulation environment with the actual environment, we calculated the waiting time in each environment. "Actual" denotes the waiting time under the actual environment, and "Simulation" denotes the waiting time under the simulation environment.

In this graph, as the number of provider peers increases, waiting time is reduced because their available bandwidth increased. In the simulation environments, the delivery times of the header information are not considered. Since network delay for delivering data does not occur, waiting time is shortened. For example, when the number of provider peers is three, the waiting time under the simulation and actual environment is 7.7 and 11.1 sec., respectively. The average waiting time under the actual environment is $11.1/7.7 = 1.44$ times compared to the simulation environment.

6.3   Interruption Time

We calculated the interruption time under various numbers of provider peers. The result is shown in Figure 7. The horizontal axis is the number of provider peers to which the request peer can connect. The vertical axis is the interruption time in Figure 7. In this graph, as the number of provider peers increases, interruption time is reduced. When the number of provider peers increases, since their available bandwidth increases, the number of empty data in the buffer decreases. Also, in Figure 7, when the consumption rate is 350 kbps, interruption time does not occur because the provider peer whose available bandwidth is larger than the consumption rate delivers the data.

7   Discussion

7.1   Effect of Interruption

When an interruption in playing data occurs, playing time increases. If the request peer finishes receiving the data before the starting time of playing it, it can play all of the data without interruptions. In DeSPerS, we can play a piece of data by buffering it for about 10 sec. of playing time. Therefore, when the request peer finishes receiving all of the data within $60 + 10 = 70$ sec., it can play the data without interruptions until the end.

7.2   Scheduling Methods in DeSPerS

In the WRPS method, the delivery schedule is set before starting to receive data. When the provider peer whose receiving rate is low delivers the next segment during the interruption, since an interruption might occurs, receiving time increases, and the possibilities of an interruption occurring become higher.

8   Conclusion

In this paper, we designed and implemented a P2P streaming system. Our proposed system can introduce conventional scheduling methods, and we can construct a delivering system based on the type of clients. Also, we considered these points: interruption of playing data, load balance for delivering data, and overhead for receiving them.

In the future, we will make implementations for client environments such as prefetch and fast-forwarding. In addition, we need to compare WRPS with other scheduling methods.

Acknowledgment

This research was supported in part by Grant-in-Aid for Scientific Research (A) numbered 20240007 and a grant for Kyoto University Global COE Program, "Informatics Education and Research center for Knowledge-Circulating" from the Japanese Ministry of Education, Culture, Sport, Science and Technology of Japan.

References

1. Xiang, Z., Zhang, Q., Zhu, W., Zhang, Z., Zhang, Y.-Q.: Peer-to-peer based multimedia distribution service. IEEE Trans. on Multimedia 6(2), 343–355 (2004)
2. Liu, J., Rao, S.G., Li, B., Zhang, H.: Opportunities and Challenges of Peer-to-Peer Internet Video Broadcast. Proc. of IEEE, Special Issue on Recent Advances in Distributed Multimedia Communications 96(1), 11–24 (2008)
3. Hei, X., Liu, Y., Ross, K.W.: Inferring Network-Wide Quality in P2P Live Streaming Systems. IEEE journal on Selected Areas in Communications 25(9), 1640–1654 (2007)
4. Cohen, B.: Incentives build robustness in BitTorrent. In: Proc. 1st Workshop on Economics of Peer-to-Peer Systems, P2PEcon 2003 (2003)
5. Tran, D., Hua, K., Do, T.: Zigzag: an efficient peer-to-peer scheme for media streaming. In: Proc. 22nd IEEE INFOCOM Conference, vol. 2, pp. 1283–1292 (2003)
6. Guo, Y., Suh, K., Kurose, J., Towsley, D.: A Peer-to-Peer on-demand streaming service and its performance evaluation. In: Proc. 2003 IEEE International Conference on Multimedia & Expo (ICME 2003), vol. 2, pp. 649–652 (2003)
7. Xu, D., Hefeeda, M., Hambrusch, S., Bhargava, B.: On peer-to-peer media streaming. In: Proc. 22nd International Conference on Distributed Computing Systems (ICDCS 2002), vol. 1, pp. 363–371 (2002)
8. Shah, P., Paris, J.-F.: Peer-to-Peer Multimedia Streaming Using BitTorrent. In: Proc. 26th International Performance of Computers and Communication Conference (IPCCC 2007), pp. 340–347 (2007)
9. Gotoh, Y., Yoshihisa, T., Kanazawa, M.: Method to Select Peers to Reduce Waiting Time in P2P Streaming Broadcasts. In: IADIS International Conference Telecommunications, Networks and Systems 2008 (TNS-CONF 2008), pp. 120–124 (2008)
10. Rizzo, L.: "dummynet", http://info.iet.unipi.it/~luigi/ip_dummynet/

Comparisons on Performances in MIMO Systems under Different Propagation Environments

Jun Sun and Hongbo Zhu

Institute of Communication Technology,
Key Laboratory of Wireless Communications, Jiangsu Province,
Nanjing University of Posts and telecommunications,
Nanjing, JiangSu, 210003
freyjajune@163.com

Abstract. [1] The purpose of this paper is to study how the different propagation environments as well as antenna configurations impact on the performances of space-time block coded (STBC) MIMO systems. Based on the geometrical differences such as one-ring model and elliptical model with different distributions of scatters, the comparisons on system performances are presented here. The impacts of the mean spread of the angle of arrival (AOA), the width of AOA and the antenna array configuration are included in the discussion. According to the geometrical models, analytical expressions of spatial cross-correlation functions are derived. The results show that the power efficiency and spectral efficiency are influenced differently by the antenna array configuration. So, thresholds of these impacts are found finally. Besides, a closed-form expression of a new upper bound of the ergodic capacity for STBC MIMO systems is also given here.

1   Introduction

In recent decade years, the research on the performances of the MIMO system has received much attention for its advantages inherently, especially the space time block coded (STBC) [1]-[3] MIMO systems, which integrate the techniques of spatial diversity and channel codings. It is well known that, the communication quality can be worse when the fading are correlated. The authors in [4] provided an upper bound of the capacity including the number of transmit and receive antennas, achieved by orthogonal STBC over Rayleigh channels with adaptive transmission and channel estimation errors. The error probability of STBC has been approximated first by Gozali $et.al.$ in [5] in the case of correlated Rayleigh fading, then by Femenias in [6], in the case of Nakagami fading channels.

It shows [7] that the performances of MIMO systems depend strongly on the channel characteristics, especially the spatial correlations. Meanwhile, the spatial

---

[1] This paper is supported by National 973 project[2007CB310600]; NNSF project[60432040]; NNSF project[60572024]; China Education Ministry Doctor Foundation[20050293003]; China Poster Doctor Foundation[20080441067]; Province Poster Doctor Foundation[0802017B], 863[2009AA011300].

correlation is determined by the physical environment, such as the antenna configuration and the scattering distribution. An overview of MIMO channel models can be found in [8]. The capacity of narrowband flat fading MIMO channels can be found in [9]-[10].

In this paper, we first analysis the spatial cross-correlation functions of two typical MIMO channels, the one-ring model and the elliptical model. Then, we study the impacts of the spatial cross-correlation on the ergodic capacity and BER performance in STBC MIMO systems. Meanwhile, we deduce a new upper bound of ergodic capacity for any practical application from the moment generating function (MGF) point of view.

2   System Model

The system model here is the same as that in [4]. There are n_T antenna elements at the transmitter and n_R antenna elements at the receiver. The maximum diversity gain is $K = n_T n_R$. The channel coherent time is T symbols and each symbol is transmitted with an average power E_s. The input-output relationship can be expressed as:

$$Y = Hg + V \qquad (1)$$

Where, Y is an $n_R \times T$ received signal matrix, g is an $n_T \times T$ transmitted symbols matrix and V is an $n_R \times T$ additive noise matrix whose elements are the samples of i.i.d. complex circular Gaussian random variables with zero-mean and the average power $\sigma^2 = N_0$. The element in $H = [h_{ij}]_{i,j=1}^{n_R, n_T}$ is a complex gain of one realization of the random variable $h_{ij}, i = 1, \cdots, n_R, j = 1, \cdots, n_T$. The function $h_{ij}(t)$ is a typical impulse response of a narrowband linear, quasi-stationary, multipath fading environment in MIMO systems. The effective output of CSNR at sample point η at the receiver in STBC MIMO systems is given by

$$\gamma = \frac{\bar{\gamma}}{n_T R_c} \|H_\eta\|_F^2 \qquad (2)$$

Where, $\bar{\gamma} = E_s/N_0$ is the average CSNR per receive antenna and R_c is the code rate of STBC which is defined as the rate of the input signal symbols R and T. Generally, $R_c \leq 1$ and here $R_c = 1$. The factor $\|H_\eta\|_F$ is the Frobenius form defined by

$$\|H_\eta\|_F = \sqrt{\sum_{i=1}^{n_R} \sum_{j=1}^{n_T} |h_{i,j}|^2} = \sqrt{trace(H_\eta H_\eta^H)} \qquad (3)$$

When $p_{\zeta_\eta}(\zeta_\eta)$ is the PDF of the variable $\zeta_\eta = \|H_\eta\|_F^2$, the MGF of ζ_η can be defined as [11]

$$M_{\zeta_\eta}(s) = E\{e^{-s\zeta_\eta}\} = \int_{-\infty}^{\infty} e^{-s\zeta_\eta} p_{\zeta_\eta}(\zeta_\eta) d\zeta_\eta \qquad (4)$$

According to Luo *et al.* in [12], (4) can be written as

$$M_{\zeta_\eta}(s) = \det(I_{n_R n_T} + s\frac{\Omega}{m}\Lambda)^{-m} \qquad (5)$$

Where, $I_{n_R n_T}$ is the $n_R n_T \times n_R n_T$ identity matrix and $\Lambda = [\rho_{ij,i'j'}]$ is a positive define covariance matrix. The spatial cross correlation between $h_{ij,\eta}$ and $h_{i'j',\eta}$ at the η block can be expressed as in [8]

$$
\begin{aligned}
\rho_{ij,i'j'} &= \frac{E\{h_{ij,\eta}, h_{i'j',\eta}\}}{\sqrt{\Omega_{ij}\Omega_{i'j'}}} \\
&= \int_{-\pi}^{\pi} \exp[-j\frac{2\pi}{\lambda}\Xi_{ij,i'j',\eta}(\phi^{MT})]f_{\phi^{MT}}(\phi^{MT})d\phi^{MT}
\end{aligned}
\tag{6}
$$

Where,

$$
\Omega_{ij} = E\{|h_{ij,\eta}|^2\} = \sum_{q=1}^{m}\sum_{p=1}^{I_{q,ij,\eta}} E\{|g_{pq,\eta}|^2\} = \Omega
\tag{7}
$$

And, $\Xi_{ij,i'j',\eta}(\phi^{MT})$ is the distance parameter defined in [13].

3 Channel Models

The spatial correlation coefficient in (6) changes as geometrical distribution of propagation varying. According to the rectangle method of the numerical analysis, (6) can be written as

$$
\rho_{ij,i'j'} \approx \Delta_\phi(\sum_{l=1}^{L} \exp[-j\frac{2\pi}{\lambda}\Xi_{ij,i'j',\eta}(\phi_l^{MT})]f_{\phi_l^{MT}}(\phi_l^{MT}))
\tag{8}
$$

Where, $\phi_l^{MT} = -\pi + \Delta_\phi \cdot l$, and $\Delta_\phi = 2\pi/L$ and L is the number of the samples in range $[-\pi, \pi]$. Here, we employ a 2×2 MIMO system and assume that the antenna configuration satisfies the following assumptions. The space of the transmit (receive) antenna array is d_{BS} (d_{MT}). The angle between the horizontal line and the transmit (receiver) antenna array is α_{BS} (α_{MT}).

The value of (8) depends on $\Xi_{ij,i'j',\eta}(\phi_l^{MT})$ which is determined by different geometrical models. Consider a one-ring model in [6] which is assumed that BS is elevated and not obstructed by local scatters, while MT is surrounded by an infinite number of local scatters laying on a ring. Assume that the radius of the ring is R and the distance between the BS and the MT is D. The point on the ring of the pth scatter in the qth group determined by ϕ^{MT} is S_{pq}. The distance from the center of the transmit antenna array to the point S_{pq} is $\xi^{BS}(\phi^{MT})$ which is a function of ϕ^{MT}. Similarly, the distance from the center of the receive antenna array to the point S_{pq} is R. The angle between the horizonal line and ξ_η^{BS} (or R) is ϕ_η^{BS} (or ϕ^{MT}). There are

$$
\phi_\eta^{BS} = \arctan(\frac{R \cdot \sin(\phi^{MT})}{D - R \cdot \cos(\phi^{MT})})
\tag{9}
$$

and

$$
\xi_\eta^{BS} = \sqrt{R^2 + D^2 - 2 \cdot R \cdot D \cdot \cos(\phi^{MT})}
\tag{10}
$$

When the scatters located at MT and BS as an elliptical, that is the model in [14] which has the same antenna configuration but different geometrical distribution.

The quantity R in one-ring model is replaced by the eccentricity parameter $\nu = 2a/D$ in elliptical model [14] . The parameter a presents half length of the major axis of the ellipse and D here is explained as the distance between the focal points. Then, the distances parameter can be calculated with the following changes

$$\phi_\eta^{BS} = \begin{cases} f(\phi^{MT}), 0 < \phi^{MT} \leq \phi^\nu \\ f(\phi^{MT}) + \pi, \phi^\nu < \phi^{MT} \leq 2\pi - \phi^\nu \\ f(\phi^{MT}) + 2\pi, 2\pi - \phi^\nu < \phi^{MT} \leq 2\pi \end{cases} \tag{11}$$

Where,

$$f(\phi^{MT}) = \arctan(\frac{(\nu^2 - 1)\sin(\phi^{MT})}{2\nu + (\nu^2 + 1)\cos(\phi^{MT})}) \tag{12}$$

and

$$\phi^\nu = \pi - \arctan(\frac{\nu^2 - 1}{2\nu}) \tag{13}$$

For simplicity's sake, we omit the sample index η in the following sections.

4   System Performances

The ergodic capacity of correlated Rayleigh STBC MIMO channels can be found in [15]. As shown in [6], the MGF $M_\zeta(s)$ of $\|H\|_F^2$ can be expressed as

$$M_\zeta(s) = \prod_{n=1}^N \frac{1}{(1 + s\aleph_n)^{m\alpha_n}} \tag{14}$$

where $\aleph_n = (\Omega/m)\lambda_n$ and $\{\lambda_n\}$ is the set of N distinct eigenvalues of Λ. The parameter α_n satisfies $\sum_{n=1}^N \alpha_n = n_R n_T$. Here, we suppose the channel parameters with $m = 1, \Omega = 1$. In [15], the authors gave the ergodic capacity in nats per seconds per hertz (nats/s/Hz). Now, we deduce an upper bound on the achievable capacity for any practical application from the MGF point of view. Apply Jensen's inequality, the ergodic capacity can be written as

$$\begin{aligned} C &\leq R_c \cdot \log(1 + E\{\frac{\bar{\gamma}}{R_c \cdot n_T} \|H\|_F^2\}) \\ &= R_c \cdot \log(1 + \frac{\bar{\gamma}}{R_c \cdot n_T} E[\|H\|_F^2]) \end{aligned} \tag{15}$$

Starting with the relationship between MGF and moment functions as following,

$$E[x^n] = \frac{d^n M_x(t)}{dt^n}\Big|_{t=0} \tag{16}$$

where x is a random variable, the mean of $\|H\|_F^2$ can be calculated by

$$E[\|H\|_F^2] = \frac{dM_\zeta(s)}{ds}\Big|_{s=0} \tag{17}$$

So, the mean is

$$E[\|H\|_F^2] = \sum_{n=1}^N \lambda_n \tag{18}$$

Finally, the up bound of ergodic capacity is

$$C_{up} = R_c \cdot \log(1 + \frac{\overline{\gamma}}{R_c \cdot n_T} \sum_{n=1}^{N} \lambda_n) \tag{19}$$

Besides, the analytical expressions of the BER performance for both integral and non-integral Nakagami-m fading parameters under MPSK and MQAM modulations can be found in [6]. The average BER of a linear STBC using MPSK modulation is rewritten here for the purpose of the analysis as a representation.

$$P_b(E) = \frac{2}{\pi \max(\log_2(M),2)} \sum_{i=1}^{\max(\frac{M}{4},1)} \\ \times \int_0^{\frac{\pi}{2}} M_\varsigma(\frac{\overline{\gamma}}{n_T} \frac{\sin^2(2i-1)\frac{\pi}{M}}{\sin^2 \theta})d\theta \tag{20}$$

5   Numerical Analysis

In this section, first a series of numerical examples are presented to illustrate the influences of the antenna configuration and the propagation conditions on the spatial correlation coefficients. Then, we discuss the impacts of the eigenvalues of the channel covariance matrixes on the ergodic capacity and BER performance. Here, a 2×2 STBC MIMO system is employed. The code rate R_c, the average fading power Ω are both equal to one. The angle α_{BS} is $\pi/4$ and the angle α_{MT} is $3\pi/4$. The beamwidth Δ of $\arctan(R/D)$ is $\pi/16$ in the one-ring model. However, in the elliptical model, the eccentricity parameter $\nu = 1.5$.

BER performance. Fig.1 illustrates the influence of the antenna configuration for different channel models on the average BER performances of a $QPSK$ modulated 2×2 STBC MIMO system versus the average E_b/N_0. The capital "E" in the figure denotes an elliptical model and "O" denotes a one-ring model. A fixed spacing between the MT antenna elements $d_{12}^{MT}/\lambda = 0.3$ is assumed and $\alpha_{12}^{BS} = \pi/4, \alpha_{12}^{MT} = 3\pi/4$ for both models. Besides, the quantity Δ is $\pi/16$ for the one-ring model and ν is 1.5 for the elliptical model. The results have been found by evaluating (20) and relevant parameters. Firstly, for comparative purpose of different models, there is almost no difference of BER performance between the two models for $d_{12}^{BS} > 1$ at a fixed value of d_{12}^{MT}. When $d_{12}^{BS} \le 1$, the BER performance under an elliptical channel model is better than that under a one-ring model. And the smaller the spacing is, the more obvious the difference is. This can be seen more obviously from Fig.2. Secondly, for the same model, the BER performance decreases as the separation between antenna elements decreases. This indicates the excellent accordance between the numerical results and the theoretical situation that the reliability descends because of the high space correlation of the antenna elements in MIMO systems.

For comparative purposes, we have also plotted the impact of the antenna configuration on the BER performance at MT with a fixed antenna spacing $d_{12}^{BS}/\lambda = 5$ in Fig.3. As it is readily apparent in the graph, the BER performance

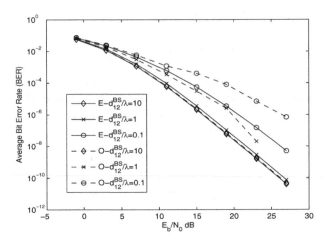

Fig. 1. The impact of the antenna configuration on the BER performance at BS I

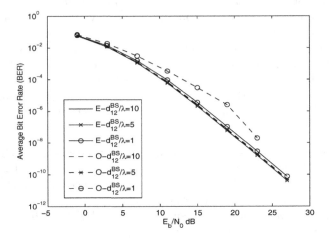

Fig. 2. The impact of the antenna configuration on the BER performance at BS II

is worse as the distance between the MT antenna elements decreases under the same channel model. And the impact is more remarkable under the one-ring model than that under the elliptical model. Similarly, there is also a bound for the affection like the situation at BS. It has almost the same BER performances for both the two models at $d_{12}^{MT} > 0.1$ with a fixed d_{12}^{BS} which is shown more clearly in Fig.4.

In order to interpret the impact of the width of AOA on BER performance, we draw the graph of BER with $d_{12}^{BS}/\lambda = 5, d_{12}^{MT}/\lambda = 0.3, M = 4$ under different value of κ in Fig.5. For the one-ring model case, the higher value of κ corresponding to the narrower width of AOA leads to higher BER performance. While for the elliptical model case, the situation is more complexity. First, the change is

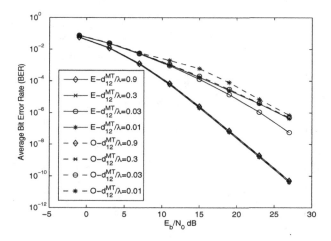

Fig. 3. The impact of the antenna configuration on the BER performance at MT I

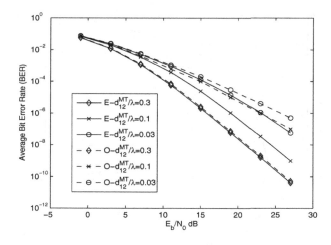

Fig. 4. The impact of the antenna configuration on the BER performance at MT II

not as remarkable as that at the one-ring case. Next, it seems that the narrower width of AOA does not bring the improvement of the BER performance.

Ergodic Capacity. In this section, we compare the ergodic capacity of the up bounds defined in [15] and (19) in Fig.6. The line denoted by 'Up Bound' is derived from [15] and the other two lines are derived from (19). It is clear that the capacity is almost independent on the antenna configuration and it is almost same under different models when the number of antenna elements and the rate of STBC are fixed. That is, the eigenvalues of different channel variance matrix has little impact on the bounds of ergodic capacity. Because the sum of them is

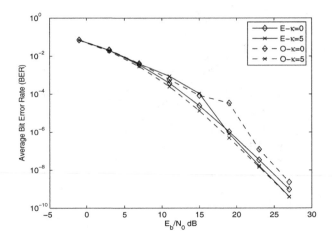

Fig. 5. BER performance comparison with $\kappa = 5$

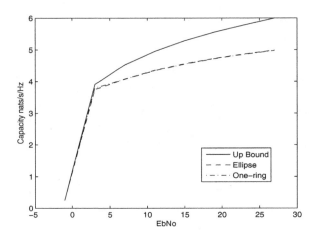

Fig. 6. The comparison of the ergodic capacity

always constant and equal to $n_T n_R$ according to (19). This result is similar to that in [15]. Besides, the new bound defined in (19) is upper than that in [15].

Efficiency versus Reliability. In order to interpret the influence of the communication conditions on the two important quality components, i.e., the efficiency and the reliability clearly, we show it in Fig.7. In this figure, the real line presents the up bound of the ergodic capacity derived from (19). We first show the impact of the M-PSK on the quality components in the same MIMO systems under different channel models. Then, the affect of the antenna configuration is discussed. Obviously, the systems using QPSK modulation have the

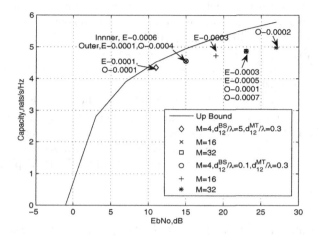

Fig. 7. Simulation Results

same efficiency and reliability under both the one-ring model and the elliptical model, which is denoted by the diamond dot in the figure. When the distance between the antenna elements at BS is shortened, the efficiency increases
($E - 0.0001, O - 0.0001$ and the corresponding capacity is 4.3517 and 4.3443,
respectively.) for both channel models denoted by the circle dot in the figure,
but the reliability under the one-ring model decreases ($E - 0.0001, O - 0.0004$).
The corresponding capacity is 4.5604 and 4.5524, respectively. The same thing
happens using other higher modulations, such as the multiplication sign and the
crisscross dot in the graph derived from 16-PSK. Besides, for a certain model such
as an elliptical model, it requires more bigger SNR in order to obtain the same
BER performance if the system wants to use a higher modulation ($E - 0.0003$
denoted by crisscross dot and $E - 0.0003$ denoted by star dot). When the spacing between the antenna elements decreases, it also requires more SNR in order
to keep the same efficiency and reliability quality for a system under one-ring
models ($O - 0.0001$ denoted by square dot and $O - 0.0002$ denoted by star dot).
It indicates again that the high space relation reduces the system performance.

6   Conclusion

From the analysis and the numerical results written above, we can make a conclusion in the following.

(i) The space correlation plays an important role in the analysis of the system
performances. The impacts of an elliptical model are more remarkable than
that of a one-ring model with the same antenna configuration;

(ii) For a certain geometrical propagation case, the antenna configuration affects system performances. In general, lower space correlation leads to better BER performance. However, there is almost no difference for the bounds
of ergodic capacity among different geometical models;

(iii) For any geometrical model, there is a threshold for the space of the antenna elements, which determined whether the distribution of scatters or the propagation conditions affect BER performance. At BS, the threshold space is about one λ and it is about 0.1λ at MT;

(iv) When the distance is below the threshold, the impacts of the geometrical conditions are primary;

(v) Different κ influence the BER performance differently. For the one-ring model case, higher κ leads to higher BER performance. However, the situation is more complexity for the elliptical case. First, the change is not as remarkable as that on one-ring case. Secondly, it seems that narrower width of AOA does not bring the improvement of the BER performance.

References

1. Aissa, S., Aniba, G.: BER Analysis of M-QAM with Packet Combining over Space-time Block Coded MIMO Fading Channels. IEEE Transactions on Wireless Communications 7(3), 799–805 (2008)

2. Ahn, K.S., Heath, R.W., Baik, H.K.: Shannon Capacity and Symbol Error Rate of Space-time Block Codes in MIMO Rayleigh Channels with Channel Estimation Error. IEEE Transactions on Wireless Communications 7(1), 324–333 (2008)

3. Yue, S., Xiang-Gen, X.: Space-time Block Codes Achieving Full Diversity with Linear Receivers. IEEE Transactions on Information Theory 54(10), 4528–4547 (2008)

4. Maaref, A., Aissa, S.: Capacity of Space-time Block Codes in MIMO Rayleigh Fading Channels with Adaptive Transmission and Estimation Errors. IEEE Trans. On Wireless Com. 4(5), 2568–2578 (2005)

5. Gozali, R., Woerner, B.D.: On the Robustness of Space-time Block Codes to Spatial Correlation. In: Proc. IEEE Vehicular Technology Conf. (VTC-S 2002), Birmingham, Al, pp. 832–836 (2002)

6. Femenias, G.: BER Performance of Linear STBC from Orthogonal Designs over MIMO Correlated Nakagami-m Fading Channels. IEEE Transactions on Vehicular Technology 53, 307–317 (2004)

7. Il-Min, K.: Exact BER Analysis of OSTBCs in Spatially Correlated MIMO Channels. IEEE Trans. On Wireless Com. 54(8), 1365–1373 (2006)

8. Yu, K., Ottersten, B.: Models for MIMO Propagation Channels: A Review. Wireless Communications and Mobile Computing, Special Issue on Adaptive Antennas and MIMO Systems 2(7), 653–666 (2002)

9. Pätzold, M., Hogstad, B.O., Youssef, N.: Modeling, Analysis, and Simulation of MIMO Mobile-to-mobile Fading Channels. IEEE Transactions on Wireless Communications 7(2), 510–520 (2008)

10. Rafiq, G., Kontorovich, V., Pätzold, M.: On the Statistical Properties of the Capacity of Spatially Correlated Nakagami-M MIMO Channels. In: IEEE Vehicular Technology Conference VTC Spring 2008, pp. 500–506 (2008)

11. Luo, J., Zeidler, J.R., McLaughlin, S.: Performance Analysis of Compact Antenna Arrays with MRC in Correlated Nakagami-fading Channels. IEEE Trans. Veh. Technol. 50, 267–277 (2001)

12. Abdi, A., Kaveh, M.: A space C time Correlation Model for Multielement Antenna Systems in Mobile Fading Channels. IEEE J. Select. Areas Commun. 20, 550–560 (2002)

13. James, A.T.: Distributions of Matrix Variate and Latent Roots Derived from Normal Samples. Ann. Math. Statist. 35, 475–501 (1964)

14. Hogstad, B.O., Pätzold, M., Chopra, A.: A Study on the Capacity of Narrow and Wideband MIMO Channel Models. In: Proc. 15th IST Mobile & Communications Summit, IST 2006, Myconos, Greece (2006)

15. Leila, M., Mischa, D., Reza Nakhai, M., Aghvami, A.H.: Closed-form Capacity Expressions of Orthogonalized Correlated MIMO Channels. IEEE Commun. Lett. 8(6), 365–367 (2004)

Combined Congestion Control and Link Selection Strategies for Delay Tolerant Interplanetary Networks

Igor Bisio, Tomaso de Cola, Fabio Lavagetto, and Mario Marchese

Abstract. In view of future dense and complex space network topologies, the management of congestion control is a prominent issue that deserves a particular attention. Given the challenging peculiarities of the interplanetary environment, this paper focused on the advantages offered by storage-based routing and on potentials of implementing Random Early Detection (RED) and Explicit Notification (ECN) mechanisms within the Delay Tolerant Network (DTN) architecture. In this light, solutions relying upon the aforementioned concepts have been designed and tested. Preliminary results show that combination of RED and ECN schemes with network-selection strategies for storage-based routing is really promising and outperform other solutions in terms of reliability, network resource utilisation and power consumption.

Keywords: Interplanetary Networks, Random Early Detection, Explicit Congestion Notification, Delay Tolerant Network architecture, Custodial Transfer.

1 Introduction

The success of the Delay Tolerant Network (DTN) architecture shown in both social applications, such as public protection and disaster relief, and deep space communications paved the way to the design of complex network infrastructures in very challenging environments. A case particularly interesting is given by interplanetary scenarios, where reliability and effectiveness of data communication, in terms of network resource utilisation and power consumption, is severely impaired by physical medium peculiarities. In fact, long propagation delays, large error ratios, asymmetric and scarce channel bandwidth pose important limitations to the performance levels that can be attained in these scenarios. Furthermore, the demand for more complex space network topologies, suited to enable a tight integration between current Internet and interplanetary networks, provides further challenges in the design of future space telecommunication infrastructures. Just to cite a few, congestion control mechanisms and management of Quality of Service (QoS) are undoubtedly important point to be taken into account. As far as the former is concerned, it is important to point out that the present space network configurations, the topology being composed of a very limited number of nodes and data transmissions being scheduled in strict advance, can hardly suffer from congestion events, which in turn are more likely to occur in the terrestrial Internet. Nevertheless, the authors of this paper argue that congestion control and QoS management issues

K. Sithamparanathan (Ed.): Psats 2009, LNICST 15, pp. 122–131, 2009.

will play an important role in future space communications, where complex network topologies are expected to be deployed as envisioned in NASA plans. In practice, a number of satellite constellations serving as relay points for storing data coming from planetary stations and for forwarding them towards Earth gathering centres via multi-hop deep space links. In this scenario, the necessity of advanced networking and communication protocols is straightforward, since use of TCP/IP suite results inappropriate due to long propagation delays and large error ratios. To this end, the features offered by protocols recommended by the Consultative Committee for Space Data Systems (CCSDS) and the Delay Tolerant Network architecture are really promising to transfer effectively data over interplanetary networks. On the one hand, CCSDS developed a protocol stack, specifically tailored to space environment, from the physical to the application layer. On the other hand, the Delay Tolerant Network working group within Internet Research Task Force (IRTF) designed an overlay protocol architecture able to cope with long delays and frequent link disruption owing to advanced store-and-forward features (i.e., *custodial transfer* option). Despite the large standardisation effort carried out by CCSDS and DTN, important implementation gaps concerning QoS and congestion control management have still to be bridged. Actually, few contributions from the space scientific community have been worked out over the last years. Akyildiz *et al.* [1] designed TP-PLANET and RCP-PLANET protocols aimed at efficiently transferring data and multimedia over deep space links: a congestion control scheme applying Additive-Increase Multiple-Decrease (AIMD) scheme is developed. Grieco *et al.* [2] propose an extension of TCP congestion control by designing a novel new rate-based scheme. A completely different approach is instead pursued by Bureleigh *et al.* [3], who developed a new congestion control scheme relying upon main findings of economics theory, in terms of portfolio and investment of assets. An important contribution to congestion control schemes suited to delay tolerant networks can be found in [4], where the concept of alternative custodial transfer option is introduce to perform storage-based routing, which basically consists in selecting alternate next-hop depending on the storage capacity available on nodes. This concept has been further investigated in [5], where the selection of next-hop is performed by applying findings of Multi-Attribute Decision Making theory. Although the aforementioned works propose strategies that prove to be powerful to contrast congestion events, they are all based on either extensions of TCP AIMD scheme or advanced routing schemes. In this regard, this paper is aimed at developing a congestion control mechanism for interplanetary networks, relying on both storage-routing schemes and next-hop MADM selection policies, and implementing advanced Random Early Detection (RED) and Explicit Congestion Notification (ECN) mechanisms within the delay tolerant network architecture.

The remainder of this paper is structured as follows. Section II shortly focuses on the delay tolerant network architecture, by paying attention on Custodial Transfer option and service differentiation schemes. Section III illustrates the essentials of the proposed solutions in terms of ECN and RED schemes for DTNs and MADM storage-based routing strategies. Performance analysis of the proposed solutions is presented in Section IV, whereas final remarks and conclusions are drawn in Section V.

2 Delay Tolerant Network (DTN) Architecture

The Delay Tolerant Network architecture has been standardised within Internet Research Task Force (IRTF) and basically consists in the Bundle Protocol, which can implement store-and-forward operations, routing retransmission of lost information blocks, and security extensions. The bundle protocol is commonly implemented underneath the application layer (where present) and over either transport, network or data link layer. Essentially, it encapsulates the messages coming from the application layer into Bundle Protocol Data Units (BPDU), hereafter referred to as *bundles*. In turn, bundles are forwarded to next-hop according to routing strategies (not defined in [6]). Successful delivery of data is checked by means of delivery options set in the BPDU header and administrative records (i.e., notifications) generally issued by either DTN next-hop or destinations. In particular, the custodial transfer option deserves some attention. Basically, it allows electing some DTN nodes as custodians, which are responsible for retransmitting bundles missing at destination. In practice, the recovery phase is implemented as stop-and-wait ARQ (Automatic Retransmission request). Correct receipt of bundles is notified by means of administrative reports (i.e., positive acknowledgments, ACKs in the following). In case a bundle is not received, no positive acknowledgments are issues turning into bundle retransmission upon ACK timeout expiration. For further details about further options available from the Bundle Protocol, the interested reader is referred to [7]. Finally, service differentiation is performed as well by the bundle protocol. Three service classes are defined (bulk, normal, expedited) corresponding to different level of priorities that scheduling algorithms should take into account during routing operations. In more detail, "bulk" class include traffic flows with the least service requirements, whereas "expedited" is for data traffic demanding for the highest priority scheduling; normal implement intermediate priority.

Concerning the protocol layers underlying the Delay Tolerant Network architecture, this work assumes the Bundle Protocol to lie over the data link layer, implementing the Licklider Transmission Protocol (LTP). The physical layer implements protocols specified by CCSDS, such as Telemetry, Telecommand and Proximity-1, whose choice depends on the characteristics of the transmission link (deep space or proximity).

3 The Integrated Framework

A. Congestion Control and Service Differentiation Issues

Future space networks are expected to integrate with the terrestrial Internet and hence to carry data flows, characterised by different service targets, expressed in terms of packet loss rate, throughput, delivery delay and jitter. In the case of interplanetary scenarios, this differentiation can be applied to some extent since data communications are affected by long propagation delays. Actually, in this context, it is more appealing to focus the attention on just reliability and speed of data transfer. In this perspective, it is possible to distinguish between data flows requiring either 1) shortest delivery delay or 2) zero information loss probability. In this light, it is immediate to recognise that these two classes can be implemented in the Bundle

Protocol in terms of priority classes. In more detail, data flow requiring shortest delivery delay will be classified as "expedited". Instead, data flows with strict reliability constraints belong to the "normal" class; besides, zero information probability loss constraint is targeted by enabling the custodial transfer option on DTN nodes. It is immediate to recognise that matching service requirements is strictly dependent of the probability of congestion events occurring on DTN nodes, in terms of buffer overflow at the bundle protocol layers. These events have two main consequences. On the one hand, the last queued bundles show long waiting times before being forwarded to the next hop, thus implying even longer delivery delays. On the other hand, congestion events give rise to bundle dropping, thus increasing the information loss probability. In order to cope with these performance impairments, two complimentary mechanisms are considered.

Firstly, the use of Random Early Detection (RED, [8]) at the bundle protocol layer is proposed and applied to for "normal" bundles. In fact, within each DTN node, incoming "normal" bundles are dropped with probability p_{RED}. This mechanism is enabled as the ratio between the number of queued normal bundles (Q_{normal}) and the difference between the buffer capacity (Q_{MAX}) and the number of expedited bundles ($Q_{expedited}$) exceeds the admittance threshold RED_{thr}, which varies between 0 and 1. In more analytical detail, if

$$\frac{Q_{normal}}{Q_{MAX} - Q_{expedited}} > RED_{thr} \qquad (1)$$

the normal bundles are dropped with the mentioned probability p_{RED}, which is an increasing quantity with the ratio reported in the first member of equation (1). In case of dropping event, the total number of refused normal bundles D_{normal} is increased.

Secondly, the use of Explicit Congestion Notification (ECN, [9]) is implemented at the bundle layer protocol and applied to "expedited" bundles. In practice, if the ratio between the number of queued "expedited" bundles and the difference between the buffer capacity and the number of normal bundles exceeds the admittance threshold ECN_{thr}, which again varies between 0 and 1, the ECN flag properly defined within the BPDU header is set to one and the number of marked bundles $M_{expedited}$ is increased. Similarly to the RED case, from the analytical viewpoint, if

$$\frac{Q_{expedited}}{Q_{MAX} - Q_{normal}} > ECN_{thr} \qquad (2)$$

the expedited bundles are, in this case, marked with a probability p_{ECN}, which is an increasing quantity with the ratio reported in the first member of equation (2).

Finally, an indicator of persistent congestion, CP, evaluated as sum of D_{normal} and $M_{expedited}$ is defined to track the congestion state of buffers.

B.   MADM Storage-based Routing Scheme

It is straightforward to figure out than in case of persistent congestion events, the only use of the above described techniques relying upon RED and ECN schemes is not sufficient. In addition to these, also advanced routing strategies aimed at prevent congestion event have to be considered. In this perspective, the advantages offered by storage-based routing seem attracting. Loosely speaking, the idea of this approach is to move bundles already stored in a DTN node showing almost-congested buffers to other DTN nodes, whose available buffer capacity is larger. As partially explored in [5], the selection of the next-hop is of fundamental importance to attain satisfactory performance levels, defined in terms of appropriate QoS metrics. This can be achieved by pursuing a Multi-Attribute Decision Making based approach [5] in order to deal effectively with performance metrics that can be in contrast one with another, such as power consumption and information loss rate (i.e., reducing the former leads to the increase of the latter). In practice decision about the next-hop selection is performed hop-by-hop by DTN nodes, where a Decision Maker (DM) entity is implemented.

In the following the next-hop selection criteria [5] have been quickly revised for the sake of completeness. Let index $k \in [1, K]$ identify the metrics (e.g., bundle layer buffer occupancy, bandwidth availability), $j \in [1, J]$ any possible Next-Hop (selection *alternatives*) for a generic node n. Let each $DM^{(n)}$ be characterised by a decision matrix: $X_{jk}^n(t)$ is the normalized value of the metric k measured at the time instant t for the node n when Next-Hop j is used. On the basis of the available measures, the decision makers will compute the most appropriate next-hop by applying specific algorithms. Here, the paper just focuses on two schemes, Simple Additive Weighting (**SAW**) and Technique for Order Preference by Similarity to Ideal Solution (**TOPSIS**), derived from the MADM theory.

As far as the former is concerned, the aim is to minimize the sum of all the attributes of interest. In practice, amongst the J alternatives, the selection algorithm chooses the Next-Hop denoted as $j_{opt}^{n,SAW}(t)$, such as to minimize the sum of all attributes:

$$j_{opt}^{n,SAW}(t) = \left\{ j^n = \arg\min_{j \in [1,J]} \sum_{k=1}^{K} X_{jk}^n \right\} \tag{3}$$

As far the latter is concerned, the aim is to find the alternative that, from a geometrical point of view, is the closest to the *utopia point* (best alternative) and the farthest from the *nadir point* (worst alternative). In more detail, the vector of utopia points $^{id}X_k^n$ is defined as:

$$^{id}X_k^n = \left\{ \begin{array}{l} X_{jk}^n : j = \arg\min_{j \in [1,J]} X_{jk}^n, \text{ for "cost" metrics} \\ X_{jk}^n : j = \arg\max_{j \in [1,J]} X_{jk}^n, \text{ for "benefit" metrics} \end{array} \right\} \tag{4}$$

On the other hand, the vector of nadir points $^{wr}X_k^n$ is defined as:

$$
^{wr}X_k^n = \begin{cases} X_{jk}^n : j = \underset{j\in[1,J]}{\arg\max}\ X_{jk}^n, \text{ for "cost" metrics} \\[2mm] X_{jk}^n : j = \underset{j\in[1,J]}{\arg\min}\ X_{jk}^n, \text{ for "benefit" metrics} \end{cases} \tag{5}
$$

Hence, the TOPSIS algorithm chooses the Next-Hop called $j_{opt}^{n,TOPSIS}(t)$ amongst the J alternatives, by minimizing the so called *Similarity to Positive-Ideal Solution*:

$$
j_{opt}^{n,TOPSIS}(t) = \left\{ j^n = \underset{j\in[1,J]}{\arg\min} \frac{S_j^{ng}}{S_j^{ps}+S_j^{ng}} \right\} \tag{6}
$$

where S_j^{ps} and S_j^{ng} are the distances, in terms of Euclidean norm, between the alternatives and the utopia point (*Positive Separation*), and between the alternatives and the nadir point (*Negative Separation*).

C. The Proposed Solutions

The solutions proposed and tested (Section IV) in this paper actually combine the ECN and RED strategies, illustrated in Section IV-A, with storage-based routing strategies inspired to MADM theory (Section IV-B). In this light, the design of possible solutions strictly depends on the choice of appropriate attribute. This work extends the range of attributes considered in [5] in order to take into account metrics that could also impact on ECN and RED performance. In more detail, the following measures have been taken into account: *i) Bundle Buffer Occupancy (BBO):* the ratio between the number of bundles stored in the bundle layer buffer and the maximum size of the buffer itself. $BBO_j^{(n)}(t)$ is the value of this attribute, valid at the time instant t, for node n, notified from its neighbour j. In short, $BBO_j^{(n)}(t) = X_{j1}^{(n)}$ and it represents a "cost" attribute. *ii) Available Bandwidth (AB):* the capacity in [bit/s] available on the links between node n and its neighbour j. As observed in the previous case: $AB_j^{(n)}(t) = X_{j2}^{(n)}$ but, here, it represents a "benefit" attribute. *iii) Transmission Time (TT):* the ratio between the bundle size (expressed in bit) and the link capacity in [bit/s] available in link between node n and its neighbour j. In this case, we have: corresponding to a "cost" attribute. *iv) Bundle Buffer Occupancy Derivative (BBOD):* the discrete derivative of the *Bundle Buffer Occupancy* for node n, at time instant t, notified from its neighbour j, defined as $BBOD_j^{(n)}(t) = (BBOD_j^{(n)}(t) - BBOD_j^{(n)}(t-T))/T$, where T is the length of the derivation window. In this case, we have: $BBOD_j^{(n)}(t) = X_{j4}^{(n)}$; it represents a "cost" attribute. This metric gives an indication on how fast the bundle buffer queue size changes over the time. *v) Congestion Persistence (CP):* is a measure of the congestions state of bundle buffer at node i, notified from its neighbour j, at time instant t, defined as $CP_j^{(n)}(t) = D_{normal,j}^{(n)}(t) + M_{expedited,j}^{(n)}(t)$ (see section III-A). In this case, it yields $CP_j^{(n)}(t) = X_{j5}^{(n)}$ and it represents a "cost" attribute.

Hence, the proposed solutions use SAW and TOPSIS algorithms, applying the above-discussed metrics. For the simplicity of notations, the solutions will be referred hereafter to as SAW-"attributes" and TOPSIS-"attributes".

4 Performance Analysis

A. Reference Scenario

The performance of protocol solutions proposed in this paper is assessed in the scenario, depicted in Fig. 1, by means of ns-2 simulator. The investigated environment is composed of two main portions: planetary (placed on the corners of Fig. 1) and backbone (centre of Fig. 1) regions. In more detail, on the one hand, each planetary region is composed of several planetary nodes (white circles) that can work as both traffic source and destination nodes. On the other hand, the backbone region is composed of several interplanetary nodes (black circles), serving as relay nodes, connected one with another through a mesh topology. Finally, the planetary regions are connected one with another through specialised gateway nodes (grey nodes), which are responsible for forwarding data towards destination through the backbone region. For the sake of exemplification, Fig.1 reports the case of 4 planetary regions, composed of two planetary nodes. In particular, nodes 0, 9, and 10 are assumed as traffic source nodes, nodes 1, 4, and 6, as destination nodes, whereas nodes 3 and 7 can both transmit and receive data. Finally, nodes from 12 to 17 belong to the backbone region, whereas nodes 2, 5, 8, and 11 are gateway nodes.

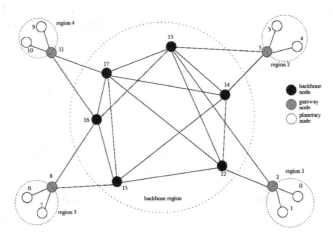

Fig. 1. The reference scenario

B. Testbed Configuration

For the sake of simplicity, the MADM-based routing capabilities have been implemented just on the interplanetary backbone nodes, whereas the other nodes implement static routing schemes. This assumption does not limit the validity of this study because, commonly, nodes either belonging to the planetary regions or serving as gateways implement large storage units, which therefore prevent from congestion events and then make the use of MADM techniques unnecessary.

Concerning the physical peculiarities of the considered network topology, the propagation delay amongst interplanetary backbone nodes has been set to 20 s. The (full-duplex) capacities of link connecting backbone and gateway nodes are summarised in Table 1 (in Kbit/s). Moreover, each node implements a bundle layer buffer size equal to 400 bundles. On the other hand, the propagation delay between planetary nodes and gateway nodes has been set to 0.5 s, whereas the available link capacity to 2 Mbit/s.

Table 1. Backbone region link capacities [KBIT/S]

Nodes	2	5	8	11	12	13	14	15	16	17
2	-	-	-	-	800	650	-	-	-	-
5	-	-	-	-	-	650	800	-	-	-
8	-	-	-	-	-	-	-	850	600	-
11	-	-	-	-	-	-	-	-	780	1000
12	800	-	-	-	-	700	700	100	-	400
13	650	650	-	-	700	-	400	-	400	400
14	-	800	-	-	700	400	-	250	-	350
15	-	-	850	-	100	-	250	-	200	150
16	-	-	600	780	-	400	-	200	-	80
17	-	-	-	1000	400	400	350	150	80	-

Constant Bit Rate (CBR) traffic sources are considered: they are kept active for 150 s of simulation and generate data bundles of 64 Kbytes at rate of 4 bundles/s, yielding 2.048 Kbit/s. The simulation time has been set to 10000 s. The traffic sources have been set on the planetary regions. In particular, nodes 3, 7 and 9 send traffic flows with *Non Custodial Transfer* option (previously indicated as expedited traffic), whereas nodes 0 and 10 inject *Custodial Transfer* traffic (called normal) into the network, in order to assess the robustness of the proposed MADM solutions. All the other planetary nodes are set as receivers. Table 2 reports the tested configuration, called Mode in the following figures and the reminder of the paper, of the combined

Table 2. Congestion control and link selection configurations

Mode	MADM Criterion	Employed Attribute(s)	Congestion Control
01	SAW	BBO	No
02	SAW	BBO	Yes
03	TOPSIS	BBO	Yes
04	SAW	BBO, BBOD	Yes
05	TOPSIS	BBO, BBOD	Yes
06	SAW	BBO, BBOD, CP	Yes
07	TOPSIS	BBO, BBOD, CP	Yes
08	SAW	BBO, CP	Yes
09	TOPSIS	BBO, CP	Yes
10	TOPSIS	BBO, AB, BBOD, CP	Yes
11	SAW	BBO, TT, BBOD, CP	Yes
12	TOPSIS	BBO, TT, BBOD, CP	Yes
13	TOPSIS	BBO, AB	Yes
14	SAW	BBO, TT	Yes
15	TOPSIS	BBO, TT	Yes

congestion control and link selection approach proposed. The first column labels the Mode, the second reports the MADM optimization criterion (chosen between SAW and TOPSIS defined in Section III-B), the third lists the attribute(s) considered in the multi-attribute optimization (formally described in Section III-C) and the last column indicates if the RED and ECN strategies (introduced in Section III-A) have been activated with thresholds $RED_{thr} = 0.7$ and $ECN_{thr} = 0.9$.

C. Results

The proposed results concern the employment of the RED and ECN strategies. Figs. 2 and 3 report a comparison between the Mode 01, which does not employ any congestion control, and Mode 02 and 03, which use the same attribute but apply different MADM criterion and, in particular, they activate the congestion control mechanisms. In more detail: Fig. 2 shows the *Bundle Loss Rate* (**BLR**), which is the ratio between the number of received and transmitted expedited bundles; Fig. 3 indicates the *Number of Retransmission* (**NR**) of normal bundles.

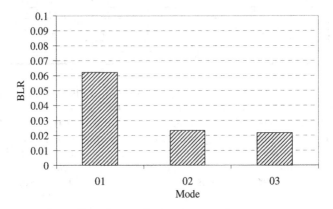

Fig. 2. BLR Comparison among Modes 01, 02 and 03

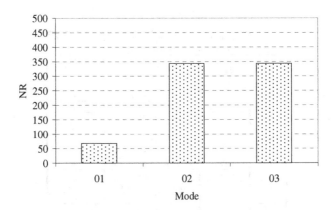

Fig. 3. NR Comparison among Modes 01, 02 and 03

When the RED and ECN strategies are active the reliability of the whole network is increased: Modes 02 and 03 guarantee a **BLR** around 2%. On the other hand, the increased reliability of the interplanetary network is paid in terms of retransmissions: the joint effect of the Custodial Transfer option and of the RED and ECN strategies increase the NR. It is mainly due to the fixed thresholds (RED_{thr} and ECN_{thr}), which impose a larger number of bundle being dropped in the network nodes. The number of retransmission increases from 68, if Mode 01 is used, to 344 when either Mode 02 or 03 are applied. In practice, the enhanced reliability and Bundle layer memory management imply, in qualitative terms, a larger power consumption because a significant number of bundles has to be retransmitted.

5 Conclusions

This work focused on a combined congestion control and link selection techniques applied to interplanetary networks. In more detail the effect of RED and ECN congestion control strategies have been associated with a MADM link selection approach. The performance analysis showed that the presence of congestion control significantly increase the interplanetary networks reliability and their association with MADM solutions are really promising, in particular in terms of Bundle Loss Rate (**BLR**), when the *Bundle Buffer Occupancy* is simultaneously optimized with the *Transmission Time*.

References

[1] Akan, Ö.B., Fang, J., Akyildiz, I.F.: TP-Planet: A reliable transport protocol for interplanetary internet. IEEE Journal on Selected Areas in Communications 22(2), 348–361 (2004)

[2] Grieco, L.A., Mascolo, S.: A congestion control algorithm for the deep space Internet. Space Communications 20(3-4), 155–160 (2005)

[3] Burleigh, S., Ramadas, M., Farrell, S.: Licklider Transmission Protocol - Motivation. IRTF Internet Draft (October 2007)

[4] Seligman, M., Fall, K., Mundur, P.: Alternative custodians for congestion control in delay tolerant networks. In: ACM SIGCOMM, Pisa, Italy (September 2006)

[5] Bisio, I., de Cola, T., Marchese, M.: Congestion Aware Routing Strategies for DTN-based Interplanetary Networks. In: IEEE GLOBECOM 2008, New Orleans, LA, USA (November-December 2008) (to appear)

[6] Cerf, V., Burleigh, S., Hook, A., Togerson, L., Durst, R., Scott, K., Fall, K., Weiss, H.: Delay Tolerant Networking Architecture. RFC 4838 (April 2007)

[7] Scott, K., Burleigh, S.: Bundle Protocol Specification. RFC 5050 (November 2007)

[8] Floyd, S., Jacobson, V.: Random Early Detection Gateways for Congestion Avoidance. IEEE/ACM Transaction on Networking 1(8), 397–413 (1993)

[9] Kuzmanovic, A.: The Power of Explicit Congestion Notification. In: ACM SIGCOMM 2005, Philadelphia, PA, USA (August 2005)

Broadband Satellite Multimedia (BSM) Security Architecture and Interworking with Performance Enhancing Proxies

H. Cruickshank[1], R. Mort[2], and M. Berioli[3]

[1] CCSR, University of Surrey, Guildford, UK
[2] Systek, Havant, UK
[3] German aerospace center (DLR), Munich, Germany

Abstract. Satellites had been successful in the past due to their wide area coverage and speedy deployment of new services especially in remote regions of Europe and the rest of the world. The future development of broadband satellite systems providing services based on the Internet Protocol (IP) needs to be stimulated by means of common standards. This paper presents the ETSI BSM PEP terminal architecture, PEP usage scenarios and security configurations for successful PEP implementations.

Keywords: PEP, TLS, IPsec, SI-SAP, TCP and BSM.

1 Introduction

Satellites have been successful in providing infrastructure for broadband telecommunications due to their wide area coverage and ability to speedily deploy new services especially in remote regions of the world. The future development of broadband satellite systems providing IP-based services needs to be stimulated through common approaches and standards where possible. The BSM work is focussed on the efficient transport of IP data streams and on how to interoperate resulting satellite networks with terrestrial IP networks. The BSM standards are being designed to use existing standards (such as DVB-RCS [1]) while remaining open to emerging standards and other available technologies (the ultimate choice is left to the market). This paper presents the ETSI BSM Performance Enhancing Proxy (PEP) architecture, which includes the satellite terminal protocol stack, PEP usage scenarios and security configurations suitable for PEP deployment.

In general, the Internet transport protocol (namely TCP) exhibits suboptimal performance due to the following satellite characteristics:

- Long feedback loops: Propagation delay from a sender to a receiver in a geosynchronous satellite network can range from 240 to 280 milliseconds. This will cause slow connection setup, slow to respond to loss and slow discovery of available bandwidth.

- Large bandwidth*delay products: TCP needs to keep a large number of packets "in flight" in order to fully utilize the satellite link.

- Asymmetric capacity: The return link capacity for carrying ACKs can have a significant impact on TCP performance.

K. Sithamparanathan (Ed.): Psats 2009, LNICST 15, pp. 132–142, 2009.

One solution is implementing end-to-end improvements techniques to TCP and HTTP. However, servers are by default unaware of the access technology used by a client. Therefore, optimizing communications for each particular last hop technology is not possible. In addition, server design principles attempt to optimize server performance rather than user experience. Thus, end-to-end techniques can provide some improvement, but cannot ensure that the best possible improvements. Therefore, these techniques are not the focus of this paper.

Another solution is to place an entity called Performance Enhancing Proxy (PEP) somewhere between the endpoints of a communication link. Among the TCP PEP proposals, one solution is represented by the splitting approach [2]. The rationale of the splitting concept is to separate the satellite portion from the rest of the network. This approach can be further be divided into two categories: Distributed PEPs where the PEP client and server are located at both ends of the satellite link. The other category is integrated PEPs with only one PEP entity residing with the satellite gateway. Typical TCP PEP improvements are:

- TCP Spoofing: Eliminates effects of satellite delay on TCPs slow start and window sizing.
- ACK Reduction: Reduces unnecessary acknowledgements to improve bandwidth efficiency.
- Flow Control: Employs network feedback to intelligently control traffic flow.
- Error Recovery: Works closely with Flow Control to recover damaged or lost packets.
- Traffic Prioritization: Classifies traffic by IP address and port and prioritizes accordingly.
- Connection Establishment Spoofing: Intelligently spoofs the TCP three-way handshake to speed up establishment of a connection.

In addition to TCP PEPs, there are other complementary solutions such as application layer PEPs, where web browsing is the major target for application PEPs. Typical application layer PEPs improvements are:

- HTTP pre-fetching: Intercepting requested Web pages, identifying Web objects referred to by the Web pages, downloading these objects in anticipation of the next user requests.
- Browser Cache Leveraging: Cache's some web pages not residing in browser cache, improving efficiency.
- Bulk Transfer Prioritization: Prioritizes bulk transfers to prevent adverse effect on other Web traffic.
- Cookie Handling: Ensures accurate painting of Web pages with the proper cookies.
- Compression: Payload compression provides increased transmission speeds. In addition, header compression for TCP, UDP, and RTP protocols results in additional bandwidth savings.
- DNS caching techniques, to further improve bandwidth utilization.

Commercial PEPs normally combined some/all the TCP and application layer techniques together such the XipLink [3], FastSat [4] and Hughes [5] PEPs.

The BSM architecture [6] provides a generic BSM protocol stack for IP services in Satellite Terminals (ST) and Gateways (GW). An important feature is the Satellite Independent Service Access Point interface or SI-SAP interface. This interface provides the BSM with a layer of abstraction for the lower layer functions. It allows the BSM protocols developed in the satellite independent layer to perform over any BSM family (specific satellite technologies). Moreover, the SI-SAP also enables the use of standard Internet protocols for example address resolution, QoS, security and network management, directly over the BSM or with minimal adaptation to BSM physical characteristics. Finally the SI-SAP even makes it possible to envisage switching from one satellite system to another and to even a non-satellite technology while preserving the BSM operator's investment in layer 3 software developments. The aim of the current work on PEPs in the Specific Task Force (STF) 344 in ETSI BSM is to describe the current solutions for PEPs in broadband multimedia satellite systems. The range of PEPs considered includes TCP accelerators, TCP header compression and HTTP proxies. The PEPs are classified in terms of ease of implementation, interworking capability with other PEPs and performance potential. The work also includes an analysis of the various PEP types/mechanisms and recommendations for the use of these PEPs in BSM networks. If the PEP design adopts a satellite-independent approach it can be used with different lower layers without requirement significant redevelopment. This has benefits for both the PEP manufacturers (by reducing the new costs and time of new developments) and also for the end-user who can migrate to a new satellite system while retaining the same or similar "known" PEP properties.

This paper is organized as follows: Section II provides an overview of BSM PEP architecture. Section III presents the past research in security systems related to PEPs. Section IV presents security solutions for BSM PEP architecture. Section V describes the detailed BAM architecture for link layer security with PEPs. Finally section VI concludes this work with a summary and outlook on related work at ETSM BSM group.

2 Overview of BSM PEP Terminal Architecture and Components

A. BSM ST and Gateway components

Figure 1 shows the combined PEP protocol stack with the BSM ST architecture. The PEP client residing with the BSM ST is called ST PEP. On the satellite network side, the ST PEP is connected to BSM ST through an Ethernet LAN. On the terrestrial network side, the ST PEP connects to hosts also in a LAN configuration.

Similarly the PEP server (called Gateway PEP) resides with the BSM gateway. The Gateway PEP has the same architecture to the ST PEP with two interfaces, one to the BSM satellite network and one to terrestrial networks. On the terrestrial networks side, the gateway PEP connects to a content server through the general Internet. Also in many configurations, the Gateway PEP will be located remotely from the BSM Gateway terminal (e.g. Gateway PEP run by an Internet service provider). More detailed on the architecture are presented in section IV.

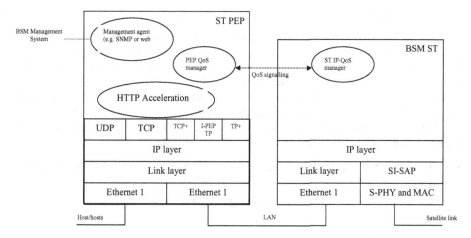

Fig. 1. BSM ST PEP

As shown in Figure 1, the transport protocol in the PEP is divided between standard TCP/UDP and PEP specific transport protocols. The PEP-specific transport protocol can be:

- A modified TCP (TCP+, such as the Hypla protocol [7]), which is used in integrated PEP configurations, where only Gateway PEP will be used (no ST PEP).

- Interoperable PEP (I-PEP) Transport Protocol (I-PEP TP) [8]. This standard protocol recommended by the I-Labs and used in distributed PEP configurations. The I-PEP TP is based on an extension to TCP termed SCPS-TP, which was produced by the Consultative Committee for Space Data Systems (CCSDS).

- Proprietary distributed Transport Protocol (TP+), where other non-standard (company specific) protocols are used.

In addition and as shown in Figure 1, The ST (or Gateway) PEPs can be managed either locally or remotely. For remote management, either SNMP or HTTP protocols can be used to communicate with the BSM management system. In both cases the PEP monitoring and configuration controls can be based on the standard MIB II and enterprise specific PEP MIBs. Also QoS signalling is needed between the ST PEP and the BSM QoS manager in the ST. Such signalling is necessary for QoS monitoring of the ST queues and adjusting rate control parameters accordingly to maximize the use of the satellite capacity. Similar signalling is needed between Gateway PEP and the BSM QoS manager in the BSM Gateway. The optimum PEP performance is expected to require a close matching between the PEP configuration and QoS of the associated lower layer bearer services. This signalling can be based on IntServ or DiffServ architectures [9] and [10] and may require cross layer signalling via the SI-SAP interface. However, the focus of this paper is on security issues and the network management and QoS issues will not be elaborated any further.

B. A typical PEP scenario

Figure 2 shows a typical PEP usage scenario with a single user behind the ST PEP (PEP client). This reflects the typical home user or home office configuration. The PEP client may be integrated with the BSM ST, or it may be a stand-alone entity separate from both the end user's device and the ST.

There can be several variations to this scenario. One variation is a multi-user scenario where the same ST PEP serves multiple users in a LAN configuration. Another variation to Figure 2 is where the Gateway PEP (PEP server) is external to the BSM Gateway (satellite terminal), motivating two different set-ups:

- PEP server may be run by a separate Internet Service Provider (ISP) on behalf of many users or
- PEP server may be operated by an enterprise on its own behalf.

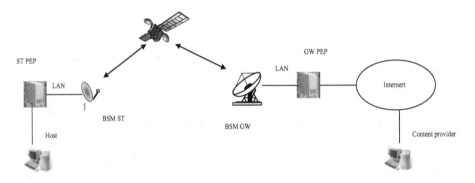

Fig. 2. A typical BSM PEP scenario

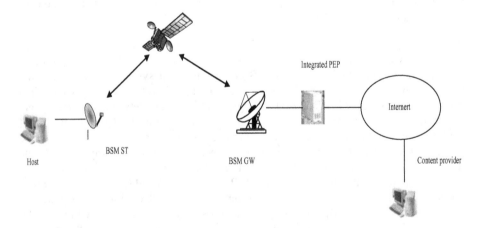

Fig. 3. Integrated PEP implemented at the BSM Gateway

A third variation is the use of multiple Gateway PEPs. The motivation here can be the presence of multiple ISPs or because performance enhancement is managed directly between user sites (VPN configuration). Here the ST PEP needs to interoperate with multiple Gateway PEPs from different vendors. This is an ideal setup for using the I-PEP protocol [8] mentioned earlier.

The previous examples showed various aspects of a distributed PEP (PEP client and server at each end of the satellite link). Figure 3 shows an example of an integrated PEP. The integrated PEP is located only at the BSM Gateway.

Here the TCP connection established among end hosts, is split in two separate connections, with the integrated PEP located at the BSM Gateway. The first connection (between the web sever and the integrated PEP makes use of the TCP standard and is terminated at the PEP. The second connection, between PEP and the final user, can exploit an enhanced TCP version compatible with a standard TCP receiver (such as the Hypla protocols [7] mentioned in section III). In comparison to a distributed PEP, integrated PEP is simpler to use but has limited enhancement capabilities.

3   Previous Research Work Related to PEP Security

Interworking between PEPs and security system has been researched in the past [11]. For example, many researchers had addressed the issue of interworking between IPsec and PEPs. One solution was the use of an intelligent switch at the PEP. As such, the PEP provide acceleration for the unencrypted packets, while the encrypted packets are allowed to bypass the PEP. With this approach, the applications can choose between security and performance, but both are not obtainable together.

Transport Friendly ESP (TF-ESP) or Modified ESP (M-ESP) [11] proposes a modification to ESP header to accommodate the necessary TCP header information in the ESP header outside the scope of encryption. The mechanism proposes that the unencrypted TCP header information in ESP should be authenticated for integrity. Although this method addresses the performance issues, it exposes enough information to make the connection vulnerable to security threats [12].

The Multilayer IPSEC Protocol (ML-IPSEC) [11] proposes a multi-layer encryption scheme. The IP datagram payload is divided into zones; each zone has its own security associations and protection mechanisms. For instance, the TCP data part can be a zone, using end-to-end encryption with the keys only shared between end-hosts. The TCP header could be another zone with security associations between the source, destination and a few trusted nodes (such as PEPs). The trusted nodes can decrypt the transport layer headers to provide the performance enhancements. This mechanism ensures security and can accommodate existing performance solutions. Though the requirements are satisfied, the complexity involved is tremendous. Also, the assumption that intermediate nodes are trustworthy may not be acceptable for users preferring end-to-end security.

Some other solutions explore the use of transport layer security. Secure Socket Layer (SSL) as proposed by Netscape and later been standardized by IETF as Transport Layer Security (TLS) [13], is a transport layer mechanism that provides data security. It encrypts the user data, but not the transport layer headers, such as

TCP headers. Since the transport layer headers are in plaintext, the intermediate nodes (PEPs) can access or modify them; thereby the performance related issues can be resolved. However, it is not recommended to have TCP headers in plaintext due to security concerns [12]. Suggestions were also made to use SSL/TLS with IPsec in order to protect the header information. The use of SSL/ TLS with IPsec is not a good solution because PEP cannot function as IPSEC encrypts the TCP headers.

In summary, there is a requirement that security must be implemented in such away that allows ST and Gateway PEPs to access the transport protocol headers (such as TCP). The most negative implication of using PEPs is breaking the end-to-end semantics of a connection which disables end-to-end security usage of IPsec and TLS.

4 Security Solutions for BSM PEPs

The following subsections examine the detailed impact of transport, network and link layers security on PEP operations. The issues raised here apply to both distributed and integrated PEP solutions.

A. Interworking between PEPs and transport/application layer security systems

As shown in Figure 4, security can be implemented above the transport layer such as using the Secure Socket Layer (SSL) or its variant call Transport Layer Securiy (TLS) [13]. Also application layer security can be applied such as secure web services [14].

Transport/application layer security will work with TCP PEPs (as described in section I) because the TCP header is not encrypted by the security system. As such, the TCP PEP will function properly and seamlessly. However, if HTTP acceleration is used (application layer PEPs), then there is a problem regarding interworking with security. The reason is that application layer data will be encrypted by the security system. Hence, it will not be possible to perform techniques such as HTTP prefetching, caching and header and payload compressions (described in section I).

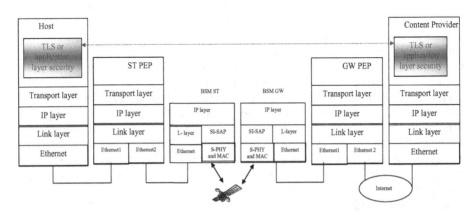

Fig. 4, 5. Distributed PEP implementation with transport/application layer security

B. Interworking between PEPs and IPsec

End-to-end network layer security (such as IPsec) will encrypt the TCP header and user data. Therefore TCP PEPs will not be able to perform techniques such as TCP spoofing, ACK reduction and flow control (described in section I). In addition, the HTTP acceleration will not be able to perform HTTP prefetching, caching and compression. The reason is the encryption of IP packets via IPsec's ESP header (in either transport or tunnel mode) renders the TCP header and payload unintelligible to the PEPs. Without being able to examine the transport or application headers, the PEP may not function optimally or at all [15]. Thus a user or network administrator must choose between using PEPs or using IPsec.

However there are some steps which can be taken to allow the use of IPsec and PEPs to coexist. If an end user can select the use of IPsec for some traffic and not for other traffic, PEP processing can be applied to the traffic sent without IPsec. Another alternative is to implement IPsec over the satellite link between the two PEPs of a distributed PEP implementation (Figure 6). This is not end-to-end use of the IPsec, but it will protect the traffic between the two PEPs.

As shown in Figure 6, PEPs can be used successfully with IPsec in tunnel mode between the BSM ST/Gateway. Here the encryption is performed on incoming traffic after the PEP operations and decryption is performed on outgoing traffic before the PEP operations. In terms of overheads, IPsec tunnel mode requires an extra IP header, where basic IPv4 header is 20 bytes and IPv6 header is 40 bytes.

Also IP multicasting over satellites can exploit the broadcast nature of satellites. However, secure multicasting with IPsec (in tunnel mode) has two more added implications: First, IP multicast becomes effectively point-to-point connections between the the IPsec tunnel ends; second manual keying only is used. Therefore, the recently published RFC 5374 (multicast extension to IPsec) provides an optional extension to IPsec to resolve these issues. However, the multicast extensions to IPsec might not be available on all BSM ST, Gateway or router equipment.

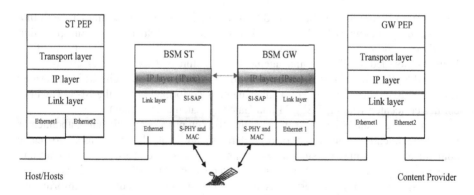

Fig. 6. Distributed PEP implementation with satellite link IPsec security

C. Interworking between PEPs and link layer security systems

As shown in Figure 7, link layer security mechanism can be used such as DVB-RCS [1] security or Unidirectional Link Encapsulation (ULE) security [16]. Here TCP and application layer PEPs will work seamlessly over the secure satellite link. The reason is TCP header and user data are handled in clear text (no encryption) in the Gateway PEP. Then, the satellite link layer security is only applied between the BSM ST and GW (satellite terminals). Finally, the TCP header and user data are handled in clear text (no encryption) in the ST PEP.

Although link layer security does not provide the desired end-to-end security, it is more efficient than using IPsec (in tunnel mode). It also can provide extra security functions that are not possible IPsec or upper layer security such user identity hiding (such as IP and MAC addresses). This allows providing strong privacy service over the satellite broadcasting link. Further details on BSM link layer security is presented in the next section.

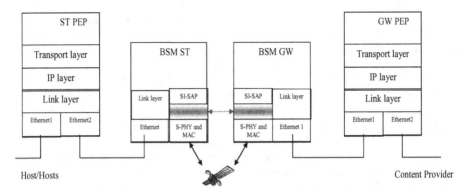

Fig. 7. Distributed PEP implementation with satellite link layer security

5   BSM Link Layer Security Architecture Suitable for PEPs

As shown in Figure 8 [15], the ST and Gateway PEPs can operate seamlessly with link layer security (below SI-SAP) such as DVB-RCS with Multi Protocol Encapsulation (MPE) or Unidirectional Lightweight Encapsulation (ULE) RFC 4326. In addition, Figure 8 provided detailed key management architecture and security interactions across the BSM SI-SAP interface. The data encryption (and data integrity check) is performed below the SI-SAP, while the key management is performed above the SI-SAP within entities co-located with the BSM ST and Gateway (satellite terminals).

Also Figure 8 show the client (user) authentication process (supplicant, authenticator and Authentication server entities), where secure link layer is used to carry authentication information (such as user name and password) between supplicant and authentication server. This authentication is independent of the PEPs operations.

The SI-U-SAP (User) interface is used to communicate secure user information (this includes TCP headers and user data). Also the client authentication messages use the SI-U-SAP interface. However, the key management information is passed through the SI-C-SAP (Control) interface, because this function is normally performed during connection establishment phase.

Both authentication server and the BSM Network manager communicate with the BSM Network Control Centre (NCC) regarding security and authorization. These

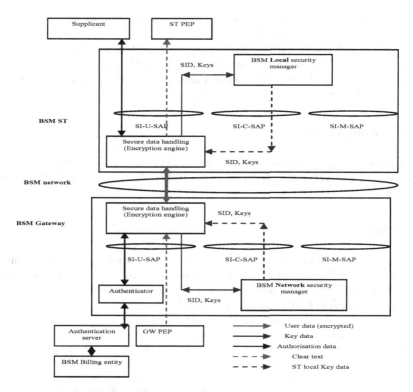

Fig. 8. Mixed link layer BSM security entities

interactions are not shown here in order to simplify the diagram. The Security association identity (SID) must be used in all security management message exchanges.

Thus link layer security can work seamless with TCP and application layer PEPs and provide strong access control to the satellite network resources.

6   Conclusion

The ETSI BSM standardisation work is focussed on the efficient transport of IP data streams and on how to interoperate resulting satellite networks with terrestrial IP networks. The paper presented the current work in ETSI BSM group in defining the PEP architecture for BSM networks. The ST/Gateway PEP protocol stack has been shown together to scenarios for distributed and integrated PEPs. Also an overview of TCP and HTTP PEP techniques and past work related to interworking between PEPs and security system are presented.

Detailed PEP and BSM terminal configurations with transport layer security (TLS), network layer (IPsec) and satellite link layer (DVB-RCS or ULE) are presented. The strengths and weakness of each solution has been analysed. The main findings of this paper is that application layer PEPs (such as HTTP accelerators) will not work with end-to-end TLS or IPsec. It will only work with link layer security.

The TCP PEP will not work with IPsec (end-to-end configuration), but it will work with TLS and link layer security.

Therefore link layer security is the most suitable solution for PEPs, where additional identity hiding (IP addresses and satellite terminal MAC addresses) can be provided. The paper presents a detailed BSM security architecture for link layer security below the BSM SI-SAP interface and key management above the SI-SAP interface.

Acknowledgement

This work was sponsored by the European Telecommunications Standards Institute (ETSI) [17] and supported by the EU Information Society Technologies SATNEX project [18].

References

[1] ETSI. Digital Video Broadcasting (DVB); DVB specification for data broadcasting. ETSI EN 301 790 V1.4.1. Interaction channel for satellite distribution systems (April 2005)

[2] IETF document: Performance Enhancing Proxies Intended to Mitigate Link-Related Degradations, RFC 3135, http://www.ietf.org

[3] http://www.xiplink.com/IMG/pdf/XipLink_Internet_over_Satellite_Optimization-R2.pdf

[4] http://www.spacebel.be/FR/Space/FastSatDataSheet.pdf

[5] http://www.direcway.com/HUGHES/Doc/0/SIKPBJS69O6KP42VCE4K4ER2BF/Hughes%20PEP_H35661_A4_LR_091206.pdf

[6] ETSI TS 102 292, Broadband Satellite Multimedia (BSM); Functional Architecture

[7] Caini, C., et al.: PEPsal: A Performance Enhancing Proxy for TCP Satellite Connections. IEEE A&E Systems Magazine (August 2007)

[8] I-PEP specifications, Issue 1a. Satlabs group recommendations (October 2005), http://www.satlabs.org

[9] ETSI TS 102 463: Broadband Satellite Multimedia (BSM); Interworking with IntServ QoS

[10] ETSI TS 102 464: Broadband Satellite Multimedia (BSM); Interworking with DiffServ QoS

[11] Obanaik, V.: Secure performance enhancing proxy: To ensure end-to-end security and enhance TCP performance over IPv6 wireless networks. Elsevier Computer Networks 50, 2225–2238 (2006)

[12] Bellovin, S.: Probable plaintext cryptanalysis of the IPSecurity protocols. In: Proceedings of the Symposium on Network and Distributed System Security (February 1997)

[13] Dierks, T., et al.: The TLS Protocol Version 1.2, RFC 5246 (August 2008)

[14] Moser, L., et al.: Building Dependable and Secure Web Services. Journal of Software 2(1) (February 2007)

[15] ETSI TS 102 465, Broadband Satellite Multimedia (BSM); Security Functional Architecture

[16] Cruickshank, H., Pillai, P., Noisternig, M.: Security requirements for the Unidirectional Lightweight Encapsulation (ULE) protocol, Internet Draft (draft-ipdvb-sec-req-09.txt) (August 2008)

[17] ETSI home page: http://portal.etsi.org/Portal_Common/home.asp

[18] Satnex project home page: http://www.satnex.de

A Satellite-Based Infrastructure Providing Broadband IP Services on Board High Speed Trains

Eros Feltrin and Elisabeth Weller

Eutelsat SA - 70 rue Balard Paris Cedex 15
efeltrin@eutelsat.fr, eweller@eutelsat.fr

Abstract. After the earlier technologies that offered satellite mobile services for civil and military applications, today's specific antenna design, modulation techniques and most powerful new generation satellites also allow a good level of performance to be achieved on-board high speed modes of transport such as aircraft and trains. This paper reports the Eutelsat's experience in the developing and deploying architecture based on a spread spectrum system in order to provide broadband connectivity on board of high speed trains. After introducing the adopted technologies, the architecture and the constraints, some results obtained from analysis, testing and measuring of the availability of the service are reported and commented upon.

1 Introduction

Two reasons explain the development of broadband communication on boats, aircraft and trains: first, the need for service and security information transmission (e.g. monitoring and alarms) and second, the need for additional public services such as Internet access and multimedia applications (video and rich content distribution on board) so as to make the mode of transport that offers the application a more attractive option for the passengers.

To provide IP based services on board of civil aircraft as well as of high speed trains, Eutelsat developed a satellite infrastructure based spread spectrum transmission and special antennas designed to meet the constraints of operating a mobile environment.

This paper provides an outline of the architecture designed to provide IP services on board of high speed trains. Such an architecture is aimed at improving the quality of the perceived service by integrating terrestrial links between the train and the ground where the satellite is not visible.

Analysis of the results of measurements performed during certain tests campaigns highlights the difficulties of the satellite transmission from a train and explains that several optimization techniques are necessary, but in so doing clearly demonstrates the effectiveness of this kind of service.

2 The Railway Environment

2.1 Mobile Satellite Communications in the High Speed Trains

In principle, railway mobile communications would benefit from having a static path, which would reduce the complexity of transmission infrastructure, e.g. using radio

K. Sithamparanathan (Ed.): Psats 2009, LNICST 15, pp. 143–152, 2009.

networking throughout the railway. Unfortunately, most parts of the high speed railway network are placed in isolated areas where a dedicated terrestrial communications infrastructure is not economically viable. For this reason satellite communications is considered the most suitable alternative for the IP services provisioning due to the possibility of the entire fleet or fleets of trains used by one or more railway companies sharing the same infrastructure.

But in this way, satellite communications on board trains must take account of several additional issues. First, the presence of persistent obstacles in the satellite's line of sight (LOS), e.g. tunnels, forests, acoustic insulators, buildings and the stations themselves, interrupts the communicability for long periods. In such cases, the problem can be solved with a vertical hand-over, i.e. by automatically switching the traffic into a local link: in this project a WiFi link has been chosen. The vertical hand-over alone does not fulfil the task of reducing the unavailability of the IP link: indeed, a very fast satellite link recovery procedure both in terms of antenna tracking and system re synchronization, has to be available at the exit of the non-LOS area in order to reduce the unavailability.

Other disturbances are caused by occasional obstacles (e.g. electrical poles, single trees and pass-overs) or periodical obstacles (e.g. the catenaries). Their effect on the traffic depends on the transport protocol adopted on top of the IP, the worst consequences being for real time and UDP based communications. Assuming that these occasional interruptions do not impact the synchronization of the on-board system, several approaches have been analyzed with a view to mitigating for these losses: on one hand, by applying the principle of time diversity for the upper layers, for example by "controlled" repetition of datagrams, which does, however, have the drawback of a reduction in efficiency. The diversity principle can be also adopted at the physical layer, whereas transmission per time slots with repetition is adopted. A second solution is the introduction of interleaving in the modulation chains, which is already present for the DVB-S and DVB-S2 standards but which has never been yet applied to the interactive channel.

Even if a good service availability can be achieved with the available technologies, other aspects (and not the least important) of the railway environment impose additional constraints and have in fact been the driving conditions for the Eutelsat architecture and system design. We refer to environmental and security aspects, which are well described railway standards.

2.2 Mechanical and Electrical Constraints

For high speed trains capable of travelling at speed up to 350 km/h, mechanical constraints are imposed above all in terms of the equipment installed both inside the cars or and in the roof.

All equipment installed on the roof of the train, primarily satellite or radio link antennas, has to introduce only a low level of aerodynamic interference, show high resistance to shocks upon impact (and strong acceleration) and to the pressure gradients at the entrance to tunnels (particular hard when two trains cross each other) and also vibrations.

Other constraints are due to the weight, volume and shape of the antenna which for security reasons has to match several specifications. For example, the satellite antenna profile has to respect a security insulation distance from the catenaries under dynamic conditions, i.e. the train roll, yaw and pitch.

Observance of all these limitations has been possible thanks to a low profile antenna design produced by *Space Engineering* which, at the same time, assures also acceptable performances in terms of EIRP and G/T.

Additionally the equipment has to be compliant with several principle dictated by the electrical environment. In particular the equipment must be compatible with DC power supply, and all its imperfections and instability, already available on board.

2.3 Electromagnetic Emission Control

Specific regulations related to satellite communications on trains have recently been defined by ETSI [1], with one standard aimed at reducing interference for the surrounding environment as well as adjacent satellites.

Selection of the satellite system, in this case based on a spread-spectrum modulation, has been fundamental for the compliancy with the ETSI indications, as well as antenna design.

3 The Satellite System

3.1 Asynchronous Spread Spectrum Access to the Satellite

Two criteria were applied when choosing the satellite system: the possibility to provide the customer with as high a throughput as possible, and the compatibility with the ETSI requirements for reducing the interference [1].

If the first condition can be matched by all the most common commercial satellite systems, the second drove the selection of a spread spectrum system. In fact, the spreading procedure contributes to the reduction of the on-axis and off-axis spurious radiation in terms of power spectral density, which is one of the main ETSI's requirements.

The *Viasat Archlight* system implements a bi-directional star topology via satellite where the inbound is based on the Viasat patented algorithms known as *Code Re-use Multiple Access* (CRMA) [2][3]. The CRMA, which has been derived by the Spread Aloha Multiple Access technique, adopt a spreading scheme where only one direct sequence code-word, which is longer then the symbol (or burst), is used by all terminals. It is hence similar to the ALOHA method for the access to a radio channel, with different remote terminals sharing the same inbound transmitting their bursts asynchronously. Thanks to the spread spectrum process, a collision of two bursts (and consequent loss of information) happens only if the first chips in the two coded bursts are overlapped and the collision probability is strongly reduced. As shown in [3], the ratio between throughput and carrier load, i.e. the efficiency of the system, grows with the spreading factor and takes the minimum of $1/2e$ (i.e. no spreading, a well known result for ALOHA). Furthermore, the use of only one code-word reduce the complexity of the demodulators, compared with a CDMA or a Spread Aloha CDMA scheme, because only one acquisition circuit (with correlation) is required for all the remote terminals.

The CRMA scheme presents a further advantage in the simplification of the time/frequency recovery algorithm during the synchronization procedure (almost without any loop), which makes the re-acquisition and re-login processes faster. Thus, in mobile applications with frequent interruption of the LOS, the capability of a fast recovery after satellite loss-of-sight enables service availability to be increased. Additionally, the reduction of the signaling complexity has a positive contribution to the global system efficiency.

The outbound of the system is a spread TDM signal (the spreading factor can be 1, 2 or 4).

Arclight improves the spectral efficiency thanks to the *Paired Carrier Multiple Access* (PCMA) [4] where the inbound and the outbound can share the same capacity. The PCMA algorithm is based on the principle that, in a case where two signals are superposed, then if the channel between transmitter and receiver can be estimated and the pattern of one of the two signals is known a priori, this can be extracted from the received composite signal in order to recover the second one.

The drawback in this kind of technology is the higher overhead required for the inbound burst identification, with the consequent reduction of efficiency offset by the reduction of the transmitted signaling (no burst time plans, bandwidth allocation request and correction messages are required).

3.2 The Low Profile Satellite Antenna

A low profile auto-tracking antenna (see Figure 1) was specifically designed by *Space Engineering* for the application on-board high speed trains. It is a dual reflector Gregorian steerable antenna.

Some optimization has been undertaken by means of limiting the geographical area within which the antenna can be used and employing restricted subset of the Eutelsat satellite (in this case the *AtlanticBird*™ fleet). The antenna performances are described in the following section (see Table 7).

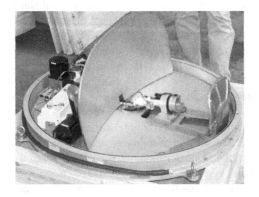

Fig. 1. The low profile satellite antenna for high speed trains (without radome)

3.3 Satellite Link Budget

3.3.1 Inbound Parameters

Table 1 to Table 3 give the details of the hypotheses from which the calculation have been done for the inbound. Two bit rates, 512 kbit/s and 1024 kbit/s, have been considered.

Table 1. Transmission parameters off the train antenna

Transmitting parameters	Values or description	
Modulation	GMSK	
Bit rate	512 kbit/s	1024 kbit/s
Code type/rate	Turbo 1/3	
G/T satellite (worst case)	+6.5 dB/K	
Spreading factor	22	12
Number of simultaneous users	21 (min)	11

Table 2. Reception parameters for the hub antenna

Receiving parameters	Values
Satellite EIRP	55.0 dBW
E/S G/T	31.2 dB/K

Table 3. Train antenna sizing

Antenna parameters calculated	Values
Transmission gain	34.0 dBi
EIRP at 512 kbit/s	40.0 dBW
EIRP at 1024 kbit/s	42.0 dBW
Required SSPA power at 512 kbit/s	4 W
Required SSPA power at 1024 kbit/s	7.9W
Clear-sky margin	0.2 dB

3.3.2 Outbound Parameters

Table 4. Transmission parameters of the fixed antenna (at the hub)

Transmitting Parameters	Value or description
Modulation	OQPSK
Bit rate	20 Mbit/s
Code type	Turbo
Code rate	1/3
G/T satellite	+9.9 dB/K
E/S EIRP	55.7 dBW

Table 5. Receiving parameters required at the train antenna

Receiving parameters	Values
XPD	25 dB
Satellite EIRP	54.2 dBW

Table 6. Train antenna sizing

Computed parameters	Values or description
Antenna G/T	10.1 dB/K
Clear-sky gain	0.0 dB

Table 4 to Table 6 report the assumptions for the outbound link budget. No spreading is adopted for the forward link.

3.3.3 The Antenna Performances

Three configurations were considered, derived from the evolution process from the prototype (configuration A), through the pre-series (configuration B) to the series foreseen (configuration C).

Table 7. Performances of the antenna

Parameters	Config. A	Config. B	Config. C
Antenna gain	30.5 dBi	33.4 dBi	33.4 dBi
XPD min	25 dB		
G/T	9 dB/K	10.5 dB/K	12 dB/K

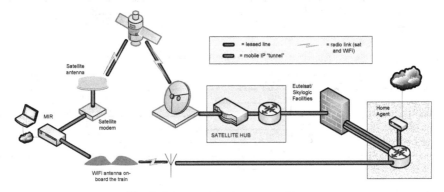

Fig. 2. Scheme of the interconnection

4 Vertical Hand-Over

When LOS is interrupted (due to a permanent obstacle), continuity of the service is assured by means of a WiFi 802.11b/g link between the train and one or more antennas. Together with the satellite antenna, this involved installing a pair of WiFi directive antennas on the roof of the train.

A mobile intelligent router (MIR) developed by Orange is responsible for switching the IP traffic into the available physical link. The MIR first assures a stable login of the WiFi subsystem on the local network and then passes the traffic on the newly created link. The position of the WiFi antennas on the ground was so as to allow the login to the new link to be completed before the satellite LOS is interrupted.

The Satellite/WiFi network layer is based on mobile IP (MIP). Satellite and WiFi are both considered part of the MIP infrastructure. The MIP Home Agent, hosted at the WiFi operator premises therefore has to be connected via a terrestrial link to the satellite hub. The MIP encapsulation/decapsulation is performed on board the train by the MIR, which plays the role of foreign agent.

As counterpart of this architecture, the TCP enhancer required to improve the satellite link performance and mitigate the effect of micro-interruptions of the link affecting the TCP connections, cannot be integrate into the satellite modem because it cannot process the encapsulated IP packets of the MIP. Thus, the TCP Performance Enhanced Proxy (PEP) is inserted behind the MIR and will process the TCP traffic passing through the satellite as well as through the WiFi. Since these two channels have very different latency and capacity, fine tuning of the PEP was necessary in order to optimize TCP through the satellite and do not interfere with the traffic when it passes through the WiFi link.

5 Tests and Measurements

5.1 The Effects on the Traffic in Non-LOS Conditions

As already stated, communications from the trains are subject to frequent loss of LOS. In this chapter, we report the results of a number of measurements that were performed during a tests campaign on board of a high speed train.

Figure 3 plots the behavior of the system over the time in the presence of interruptions. The antenna used was the pre-series model (configuration B). The first graph, the *Automatic Gain Control* (AGC) values, shows a variable proportional to the beacon level measured by the narrowband receiver of the antenna. The tracking algorithm antenna aims at maximizing this value (the periodical dropping of the AGC value due to a frequency scan used by the tracking algorithm indicates that there was perfect reception without interruptions). The second graph represents the Eb/No received at the modem (in this case the outbound used was at 3.5 Mbit/s instead of 20 Mbit/s) and gives a qualitative comparison of the effect of interruptions on the signal. The third graph shows with vertical bars the *icmp* requests having a successful reply and proves that the impact of the interruptions is rather severe for the IP packets. The

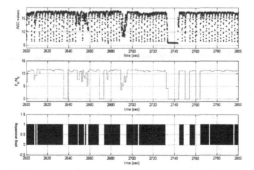

Fig. 3. Impact of the signal losses on the IP traffic (sampling in a period of 200s)

reason is due to the fact that even if the reception shows just a small attenuation, the transmission is heavily impacted. The presence of a UPC algorithm in the modem cannot solve the problem, because its reaction time is usually longer then the duration of the attenuation.

Most recent experiences have demonstrated that the effects on the TCP traffic of micro-interruption can be easily mitigated with the state-of-the-art TCP enhancer algorithms (SACK, fast recovery, accelerated slow start have been retained for the deployment on the proposed Eutelsat services). Conversely, the UDP traffic remains more sensitive to this kind of loss and its protection can be ensured only by the addition of redundancy in the transmission with the introduction of application layer FEC, as proposed in the DVB-RCS+M standard [5]. Additionally, other proprietary solutions (to be tested soon by Eutelsat) propose to mitigate the effect of short interruption with the insertion of interleaving (deepness adjustable) in the forward link coding scheme.

5.2 The Coverage Mapping

Relating the previous measurements to the geographical position (GPS coordinates) gives an idea of coverage availability.

Measurements were performed to record the level of the beacon used by the antenna for the tracking purposes and to record the geographical coordinates. Here too, this is represented by the AGC value: any unitary variation of this parameter is in fact equivalent to a 1 dB variation of the level, and recording instantaneous values of this variable corresponds to recording a trace of the fading along the railway path. Figure 4 shows a segment of the coverage measured along a high speed line (over 300 km/h). Analysis of the plot makes it possible to understand the position where the satellite link is unavailable or only attenuated, and the railway operator can thus identify the locations where the infrastructure for the secondary terrestrial link must be installed.

The same measurements enabled the aggregate availability to be defined as a function of the distance from the departing station. The aggregate availability is the ratio between the aggregate distance on which the satellite link is available and the

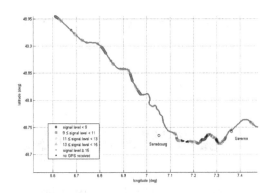

Fig. 4. Coverage representation in a segment of the train path

total distance covered. The computation was performed using the very pessimistic assumption that the satellite link is not available if there is an attenuation of 3.5 dB from the maximum. Furthermore, in the computation, a positive contribution to the aggregate availability is given only if at least two consecutive samplings proved that the satellite link was available. This assumption avoids the possibility of considering in the availability budget any isolated points at which the satellite is visible without this making a real contribution to the availability of the service.

Figure 5 shows the aggregated availability as function of the distance to the station from which the train departed and to which it returned, in a path covering both directions (in the return trip a small deviation has slightly changed the statistics). The numbers in the picture have been inserted to mark the train's passage at the same points. Note, in particular, the strong falling off of the availability between points 2 and 3 due to the presence of a long tunnel which should be equipped with WiFi for the handover purposes.

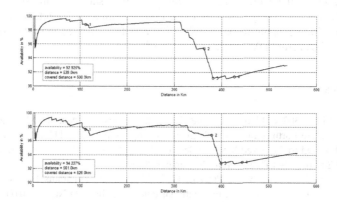

Fig. 5. Availability calculated in the same railway path covered in the two directions

Even though the aggregated availability is similar between the two paths (at the end of the path is between 93% and 94%), certain differences emerge when the two plots are compared. These differences are due to:

a.   the path is not identical, because the train runs on varying side of the track (in Italy and France on the left, in Germany on the right) and also because of the effect of the of the obstacles on the degree of fading, which is different as a function of the distance from the train;

b.   the speed is not the same in each directions which can have a different impact both on the statistics and on the tracking algorithm of the antenna;

The measurements have been performed on different paths and shows that the availability is strongly dependent on the path (it is not difficult to appreciate that certain regions in the middle of the mountains do not offer an ideal environment for satellite communications). The most recent analysis of the traffic generated on board a number of trains in commercial service, and also the feedback from customers, shows that 90% availability (and it was the case above described) is enough to make the service effective.

6 Conclusions and Future Work

Eutelsat is today beginning to deploy and operate one of the first satellite networks for mobile high speed railway communications. During a previous pre-operational phase several problems have been encountered, principally due to the extremely severe working conditions imposed by the railway environment, and certain elements have required further improvement. The positive feedbacks from customers and the results of the measurements of link availability prove that satellite is a promising solution and several activities must be planned for the future.

The first obstacle to be overcome in the future evolution of the technology is the reduction in the size of the antennas for installation on double-deckers trains (where the space on the roof is significantly reduced). Flat array antennas and the Ka band seem to be the most attractive solutions, even if a lot of work is necessary order to adapt these technologies to the railway domain.

Other targets will be the usage of new generation satellites, in particular in Ka band, with cellular coverage. In this case, both antennas and modems will have to include algorithms capable to hand-over from one foot-print to the other (as already described by the current DVB-RCS+M standard).

References

[1] Draft ETSI EN 302 448 V0.18.2 - Satellite Earth Stations and Systems (SES); Harmonized EN for satellite Earth Stations on Trains (ESTs) operating in the 11/12/14 GHz frequency bands allocated to the Fixed Satellite Service (FSS) covering essential requirements under article 3.2 of the R&TTE directive (November 2005)

[2] Miller, M.J., Dankberg, M.D., Pateros, C.N.: Method and apparatus for multiple access over a communication channel, International Patent. Publication Nr. WO 01/13534 A1, S. Francisco, CA (2000)

[3] Pateros, C.N.: Novel direct sequence spread spectrum multiple access technique. In: 21st Century Military Communications Conference Proceedings, MILCOM 2000, vol. 1, pp. 564–568 (2000)

[4] Paired Carrier Multiple Access for Satellite Communications, Mark Dankberg. In: Proceedings of Pacific Telecommunications Conference (January 1998)

[5] ETSI EN 301 790, DVB - Interaction Channel for Satellite Distribution Systems

Author Index

Printed in the United States
By Bookmasters